Petit Pattern Book

Petit Pattern Book
Scandinavian Style

Copyright ©2006 2m09cmGRAPHICS, Inc.
www.209g.com

Published in 2006 by BNN, Inc.
11F Shinjuku Square Tower Building
6-22-1 Nishi-shinjuku, Shinjuku-ku
Tokyo 163-1111 Japan
info@bnn.co.jp
www.bnn.co.jp

Art Direction: Masanari Nakayama (2m09cmGRAPHICS)
Book Design: Shota Yamagiwa (2m09cmGRAPHICS)
Pattern Design: 2m09cmGRAPHICS
Photo Assistant: Rie Kaneko
Translation: R.I.C. Publication Asia Co., Inc.

ISBN 4-86100-386-5

Printed in Japan by Shinano, Ltd.

おしゃれなパターン素材集

北欧・ファブリック

Petit Pattern Book

Scandinavian style

はじめに

「こんなパターン集がほしかった!」
いままでありそうでなかった、おしゃれな素材集の誕生です。デジタルな
のに、なんだか味のあるパターンたち。紙に出力するだけで、とってもか
わいいプリントになります。CD-ROMには、Illustrator用EPSファイルと
Photoshop用JPEGファイルで、本に掲載しているすべてのパターン
がデータ収録されているので、気に入ったパターンをそのまま使うのは
もちろん、色を変えたりサイズを変えたり、あなただけのオリジナルパタ
ーンをつくることもできます。お部屋のアクセントにしたり、デイリーの小
物をリメイクしたり、大切な人へのプレゼントを包んだり。メインに、背景
に、ピンポイントに、パターンを生かした手作りグッズで、日々の暮らしを
いっそう楽しく演出しましょう。

Introduction

"At last - the collection of patterns I wanted!"
The collection of stylish patterns, which everyone has been waiting for, is finally available. Although they are digital images they have their own personalities. You can make pretty prints just by outputting on paper. In the CD-ROM provided, EPS files for Illustrator and JPEG files for Photoshop are to be found; because they contain the data for all the patterns in the book, you can not only use any patterns you like as they are, but you can also change colors or sizes, or make your original patterns. You can use them to match the decoration of your room, to remake objects you use everyday, or as paper to wrap presents for people who are important to you. When you make original items, use the patterns to form the main part of your design, as a background, or as a focal point. They will surely liven up your everyday life.

contents

things you can make with patterns

パターンをつかったあれこれ

Petit Pattern Book
Scandinavian style

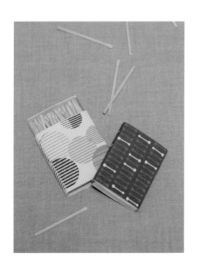

北欧・ファブリック

001〜140

Petit Pattern Book

Scandinavian style

•003 ｜ 北欧・ファブリック *Scandinavian style*

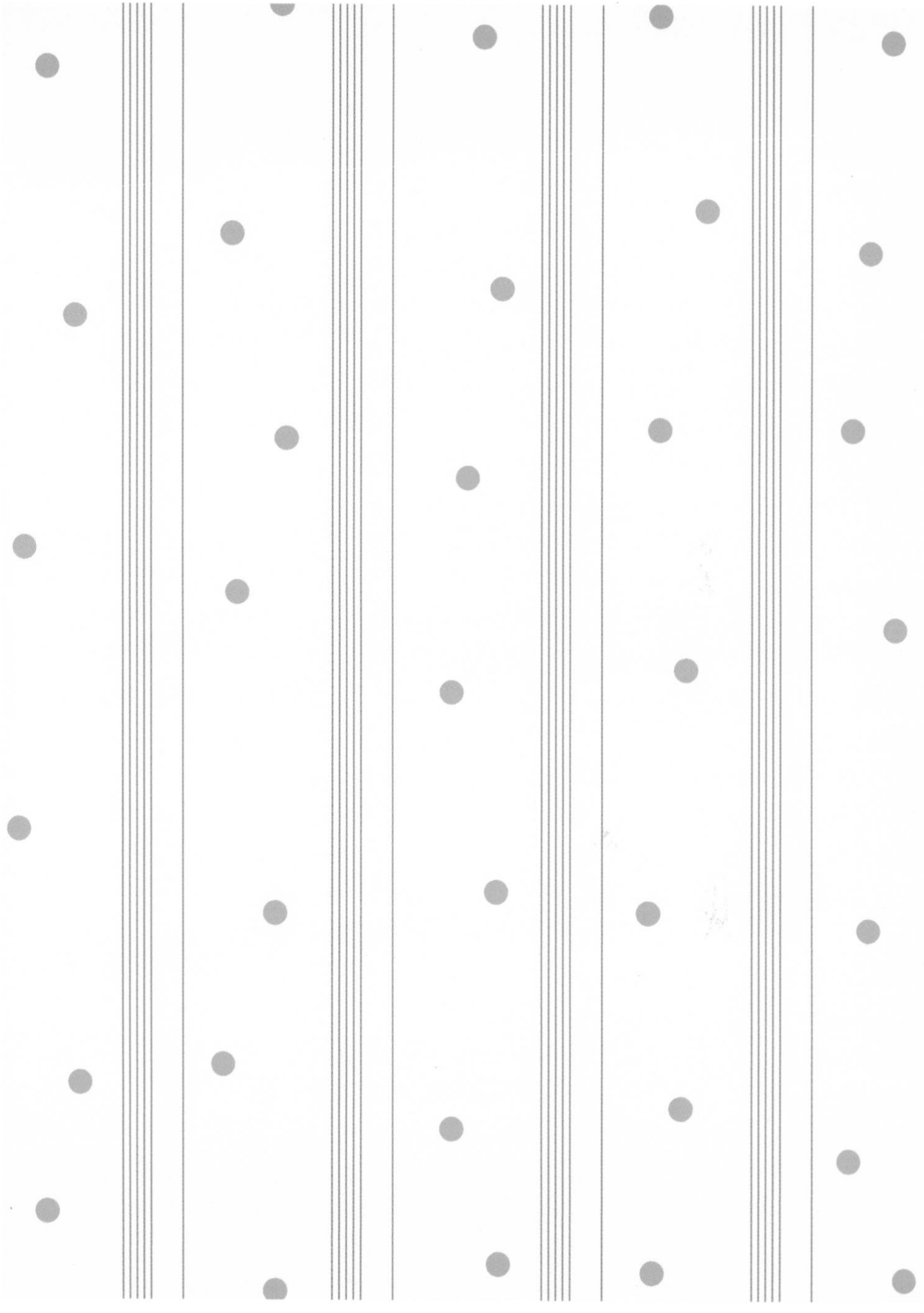

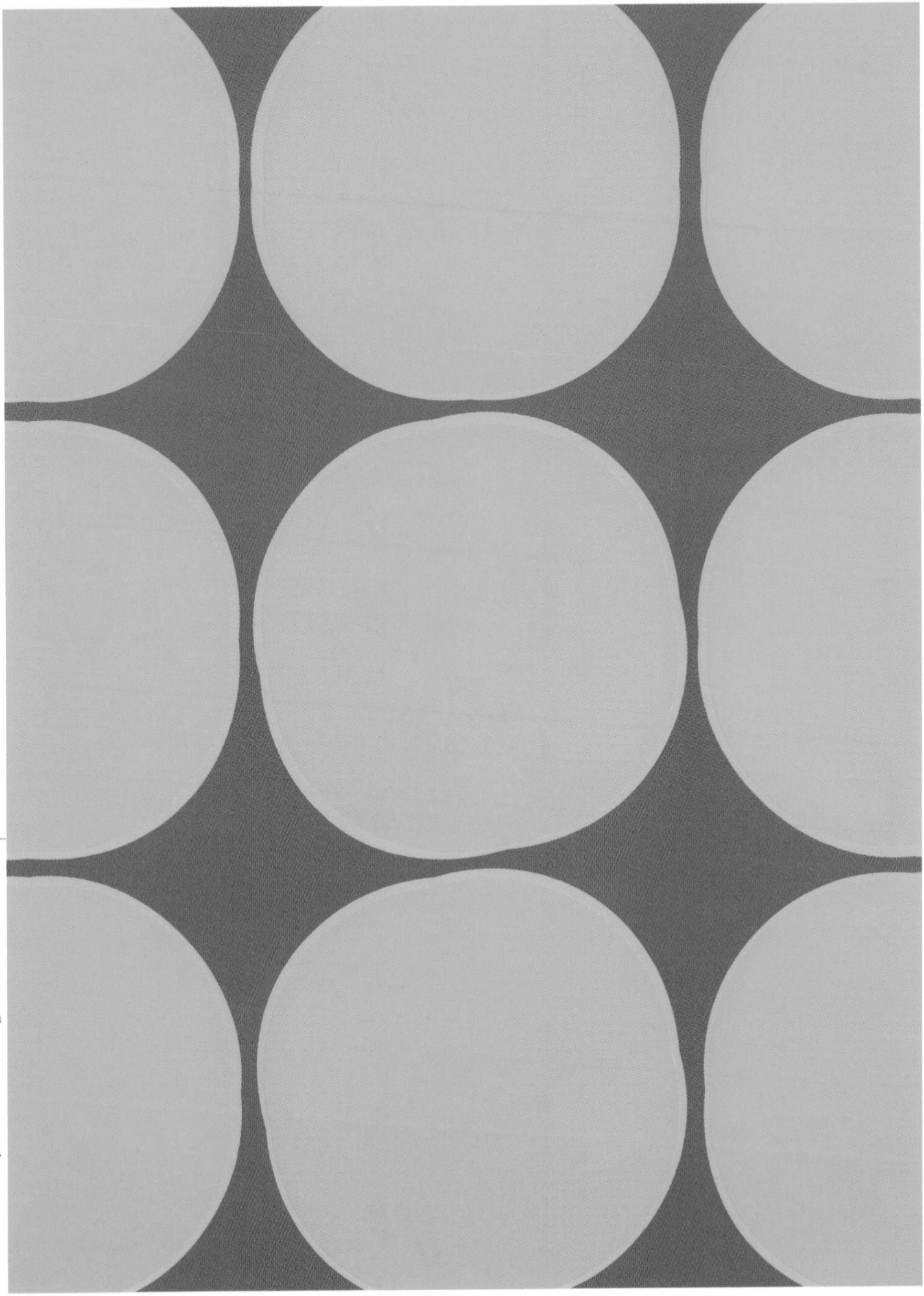

● 011　北欧・ファブリック　*Scandinavian style*

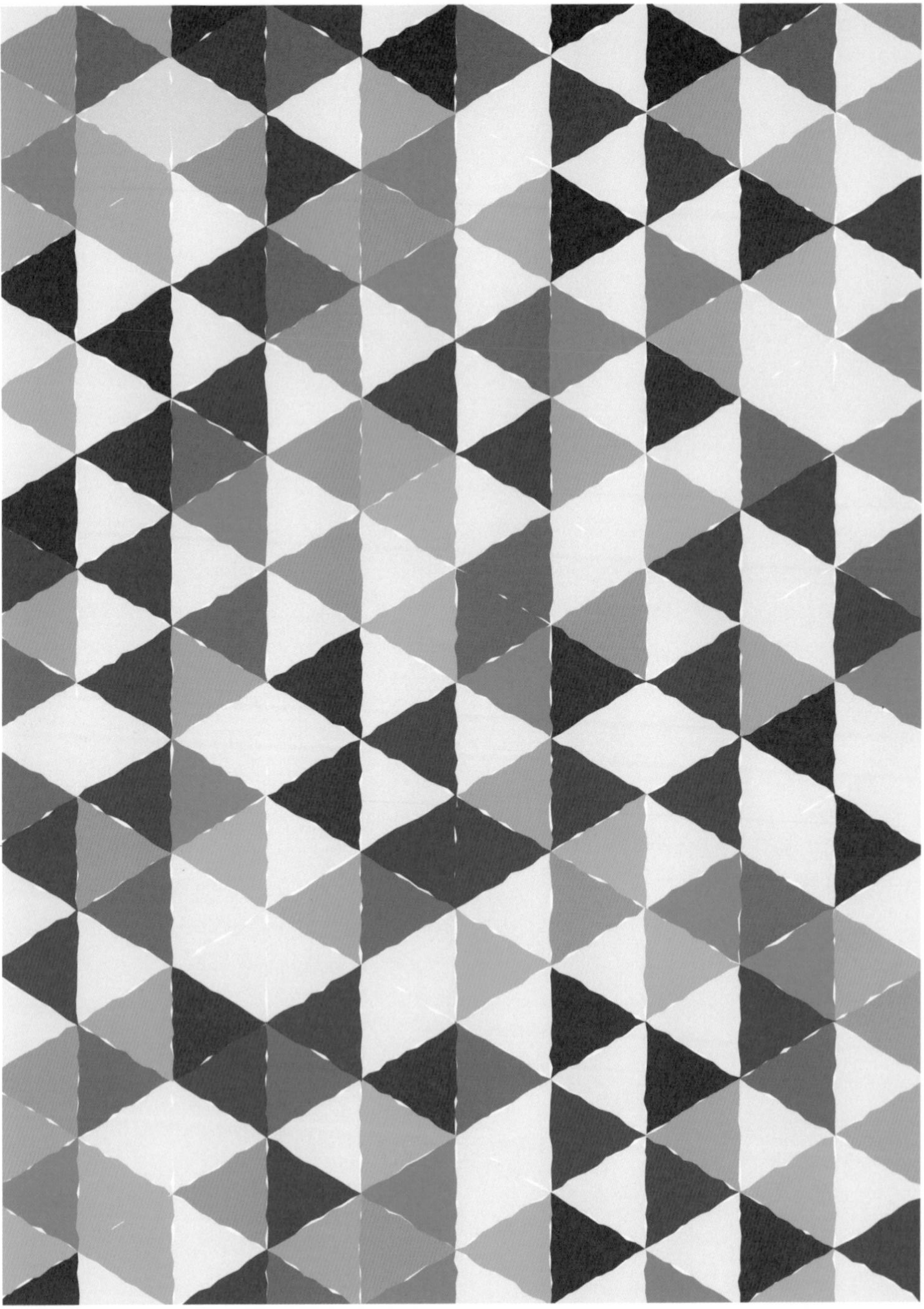

•013 北欧・ファブリック *Scandinavian style*

•014 北欧・ファブリック *Scandinavian style*

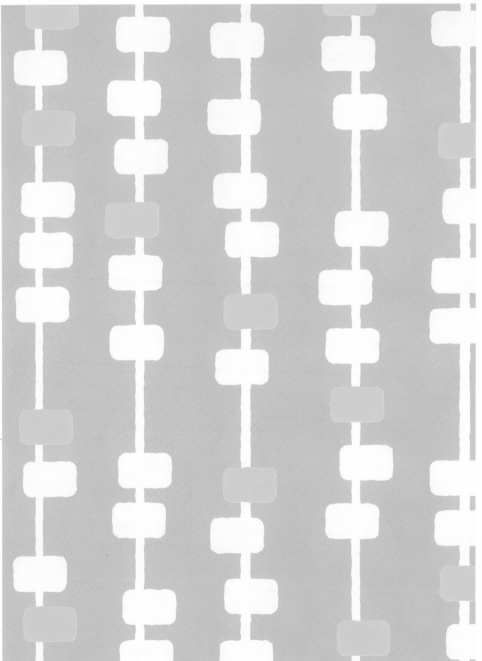

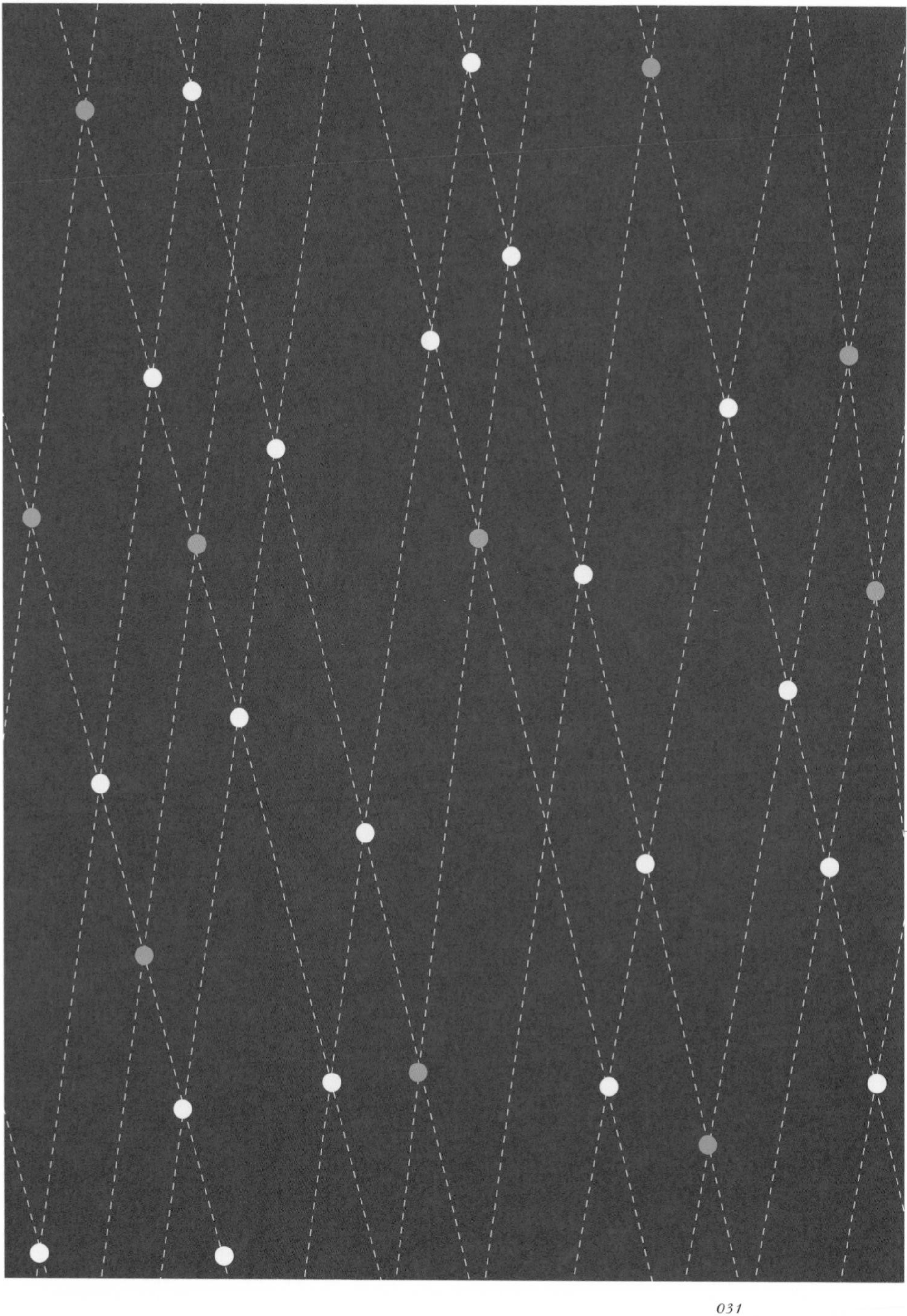

北欧・ファブリック *Scandinavian style*

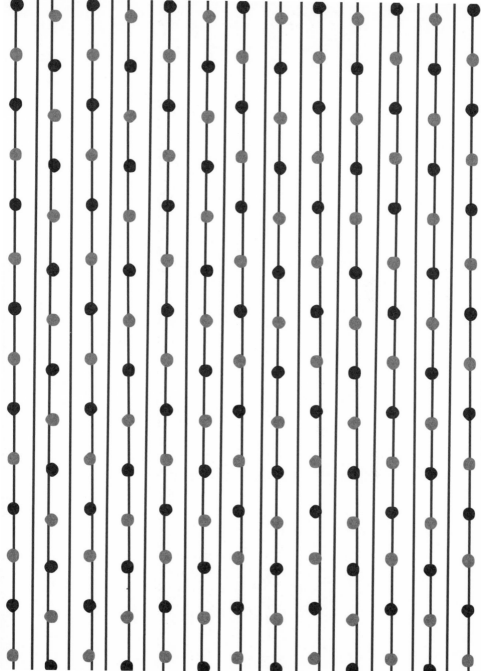

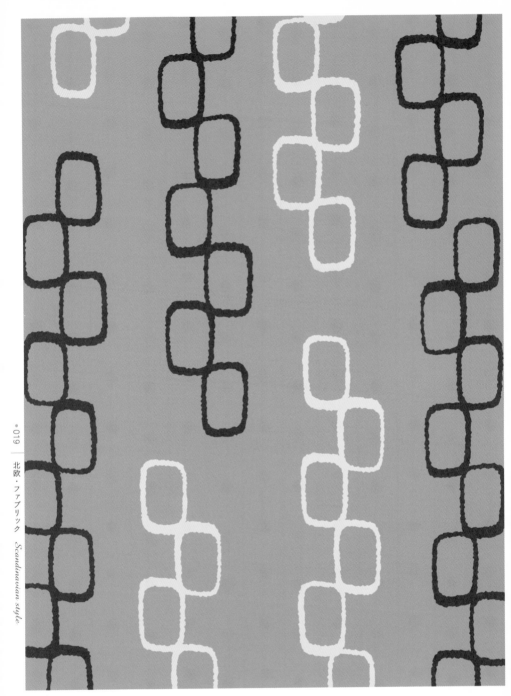

*019　北欧・ファブリック　*Scandinavian style*

● 021 北欧・ファブリック Scandinavian style

北欧・ファブリック　*Scandinavian style*

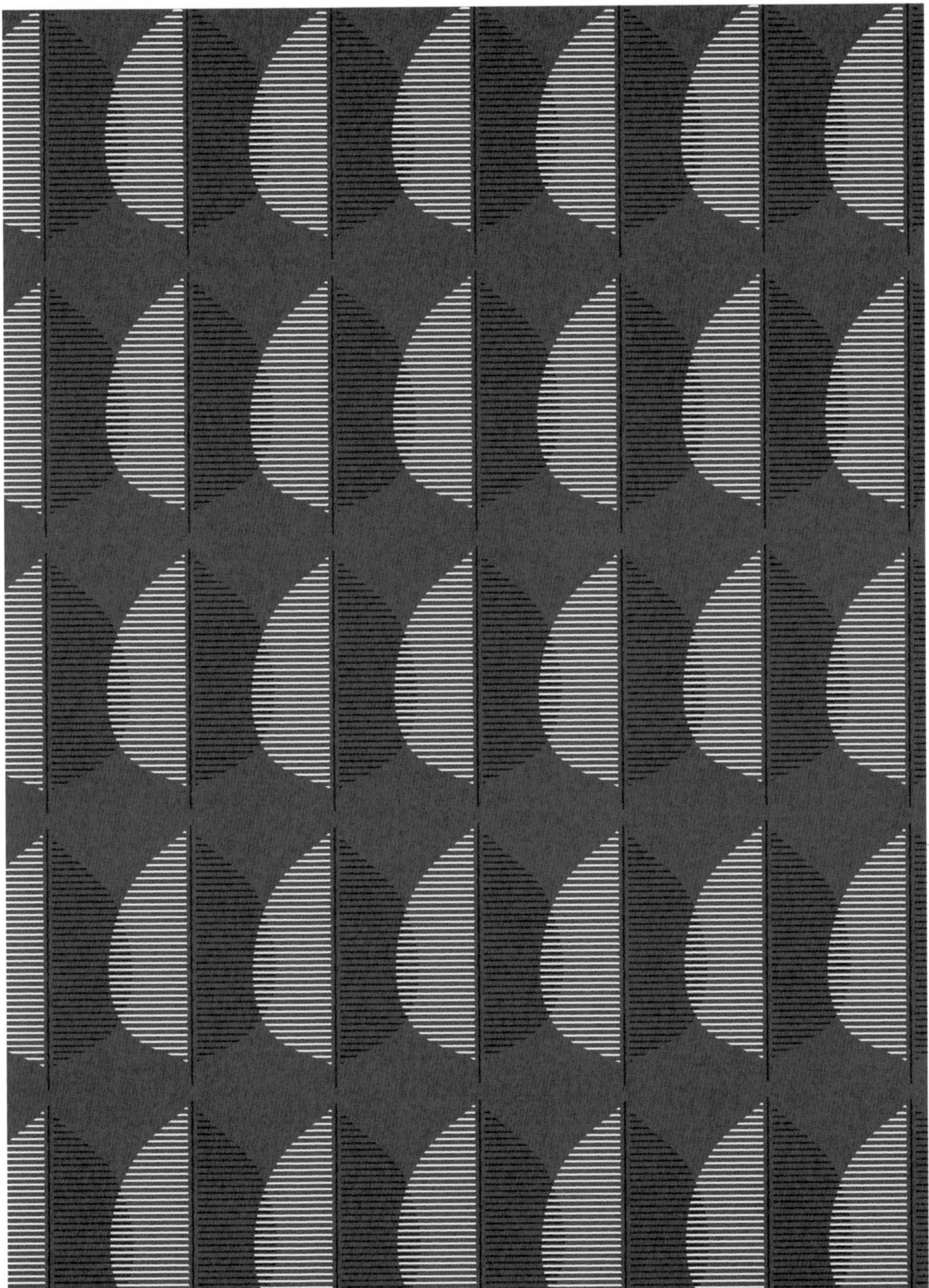

●026 北欧・ファブリック *Scandinavian style*

* 029　北欧・ファブリック　Scandinavian style

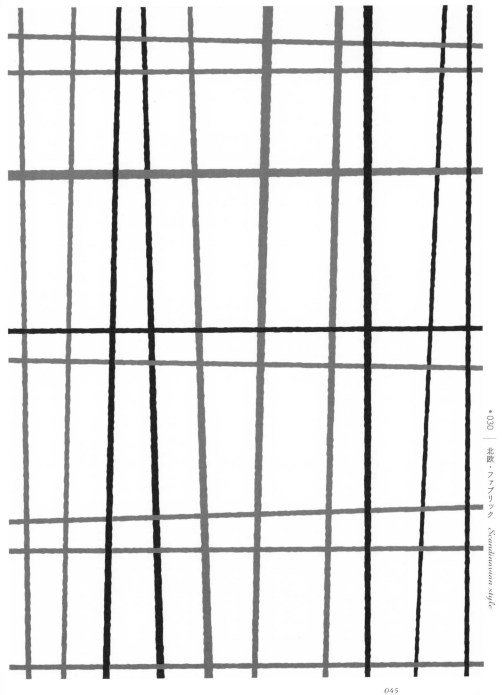

北欧・ファブリック　*Scandinavian style*

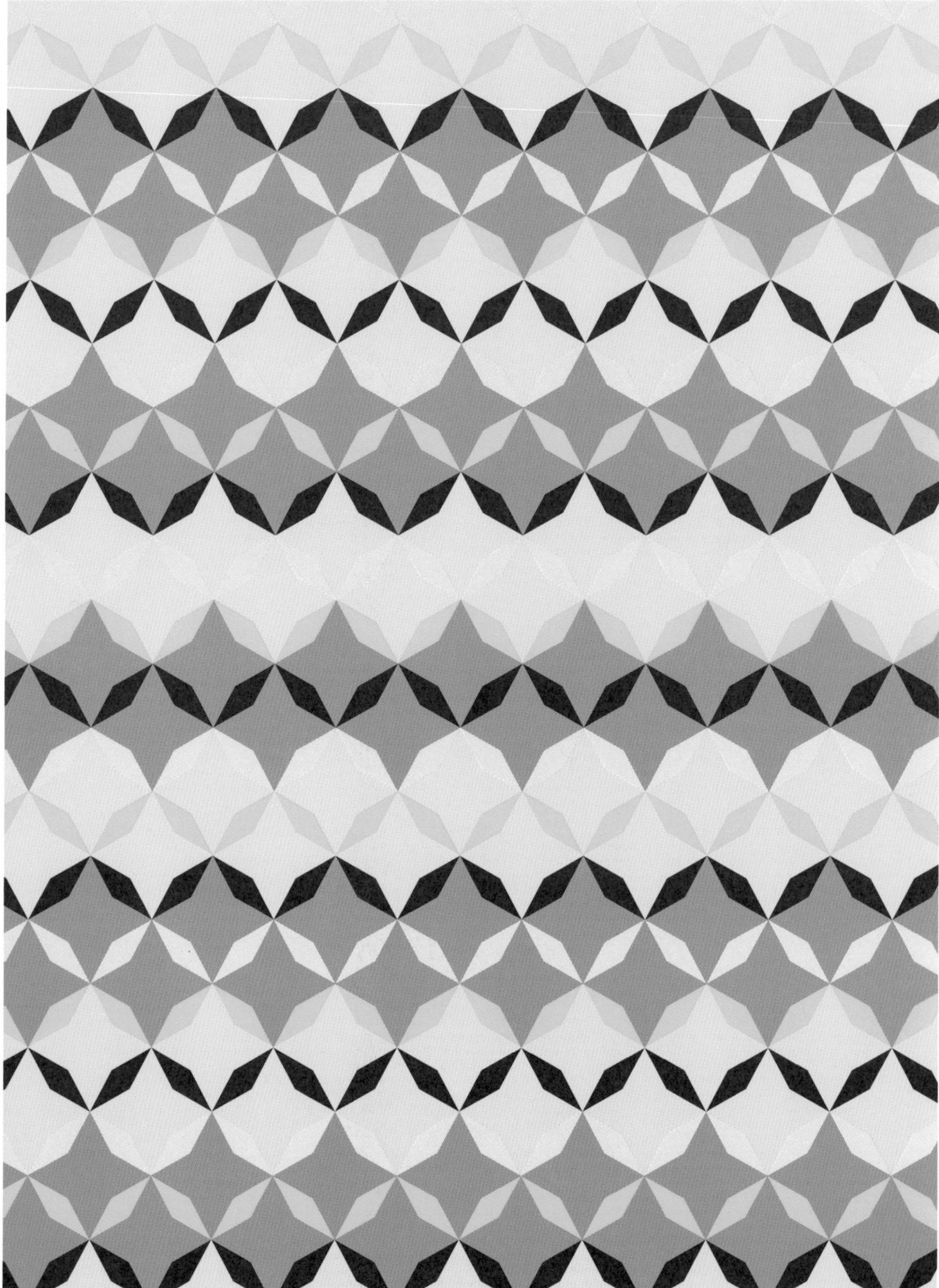

•034

北欧・ファブリック *Scandinavian style*

北欧・ファブリック *Scandinavian style*

北欧・ファブリック　*Scandinavian style*

* 043 ｜ 北欧・ファブリック *Scandinavian style*

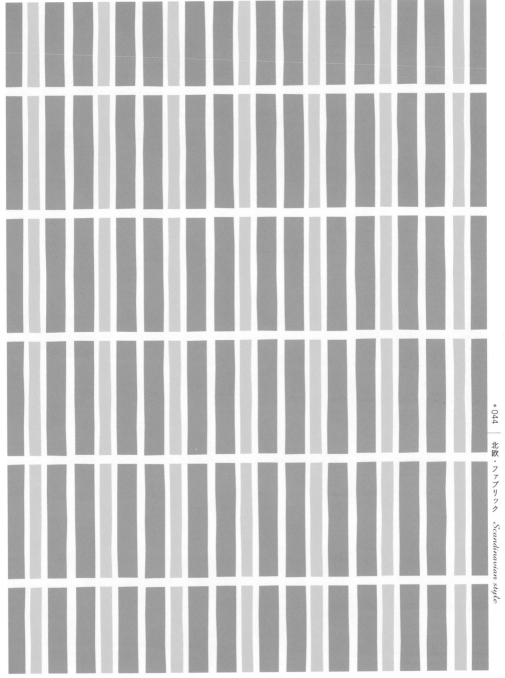

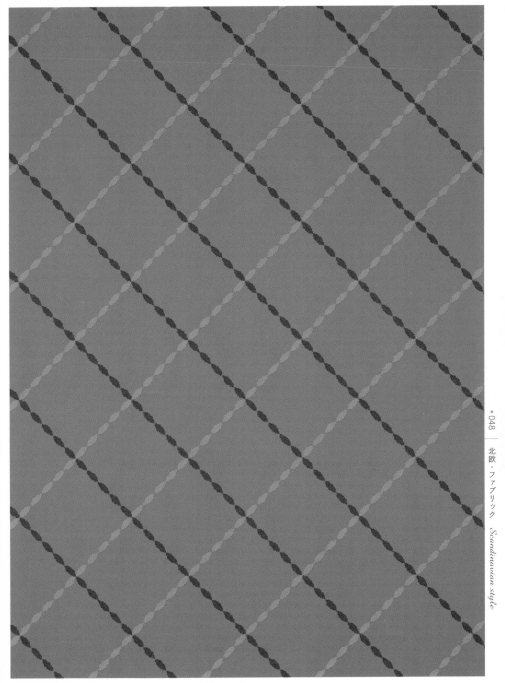

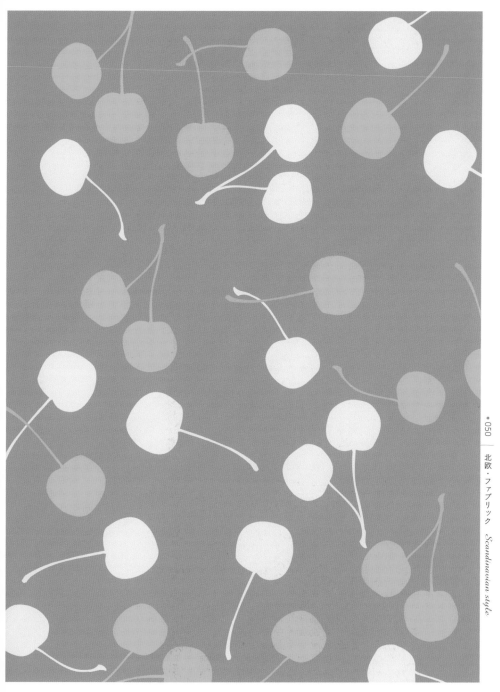

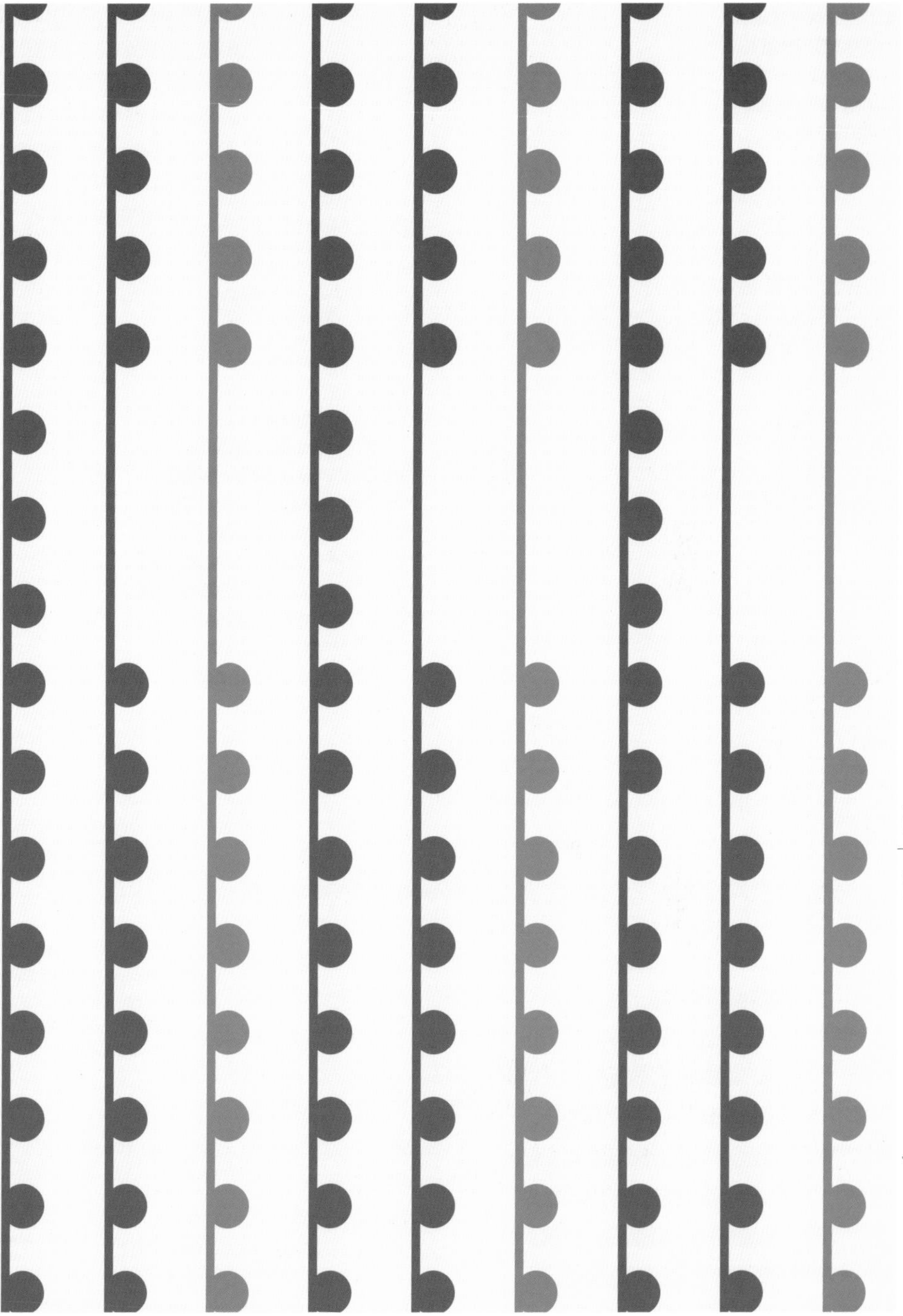

•052 北欧・ファブリック *Scandinavian style*

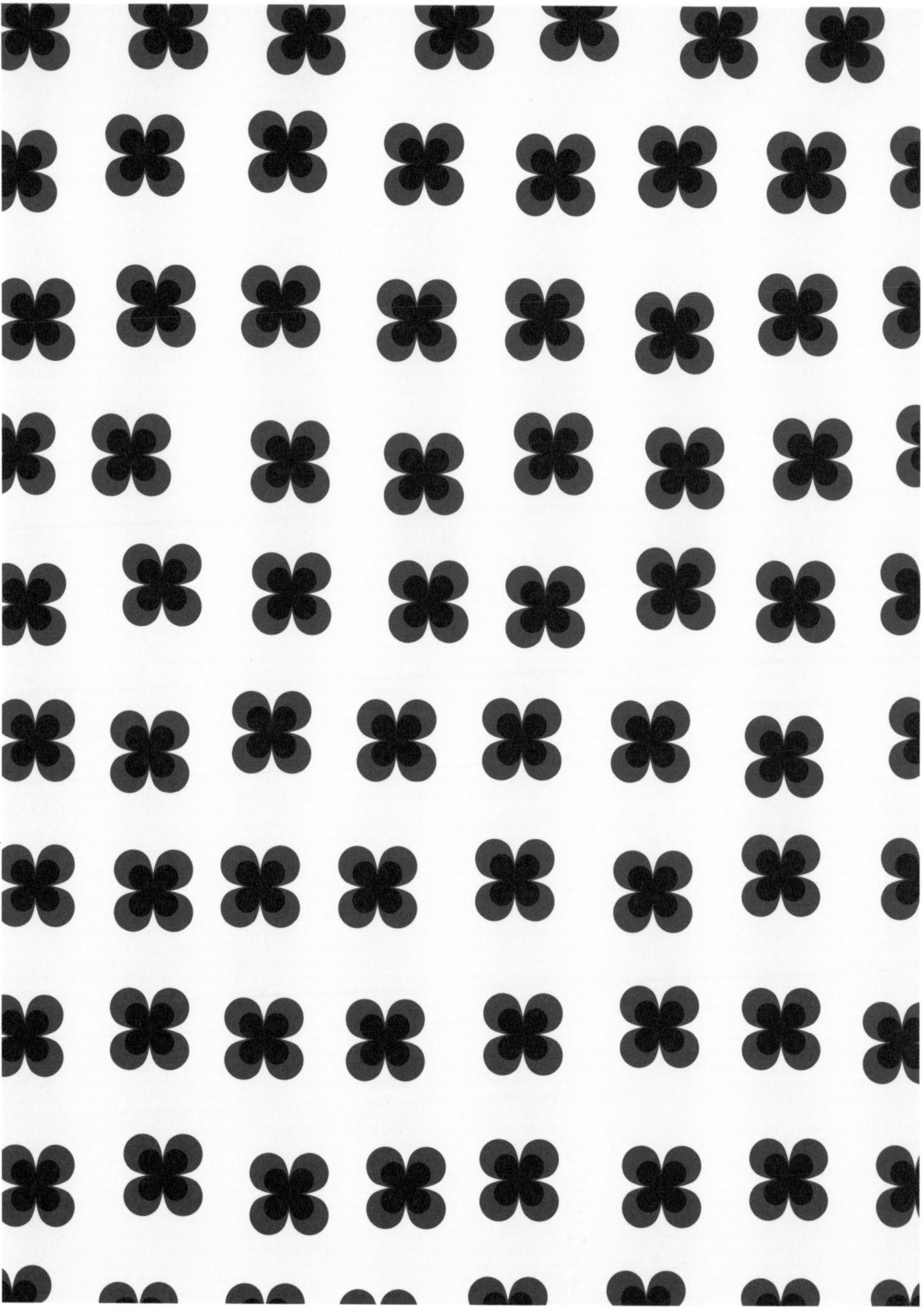

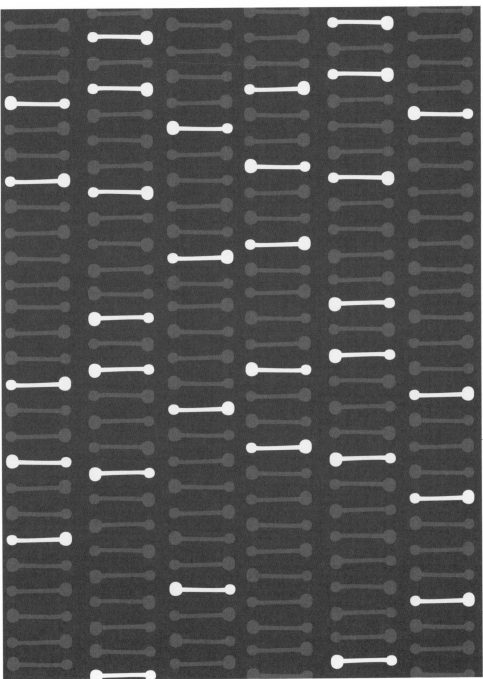

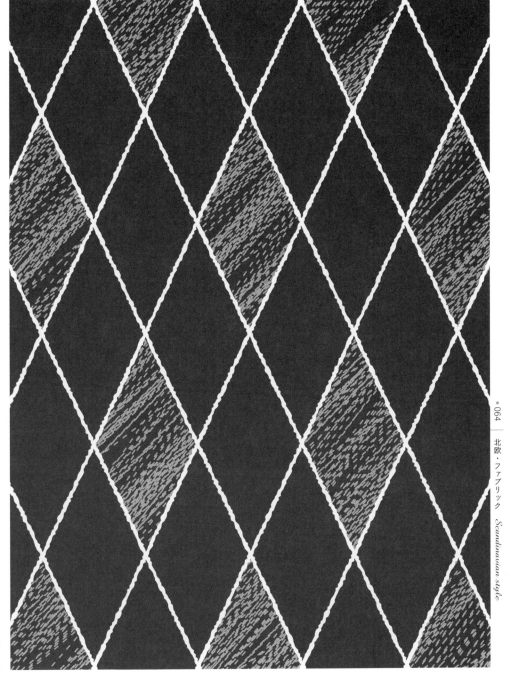

● 067 ｜ 北欧・ファブリック *Scandinavian style*

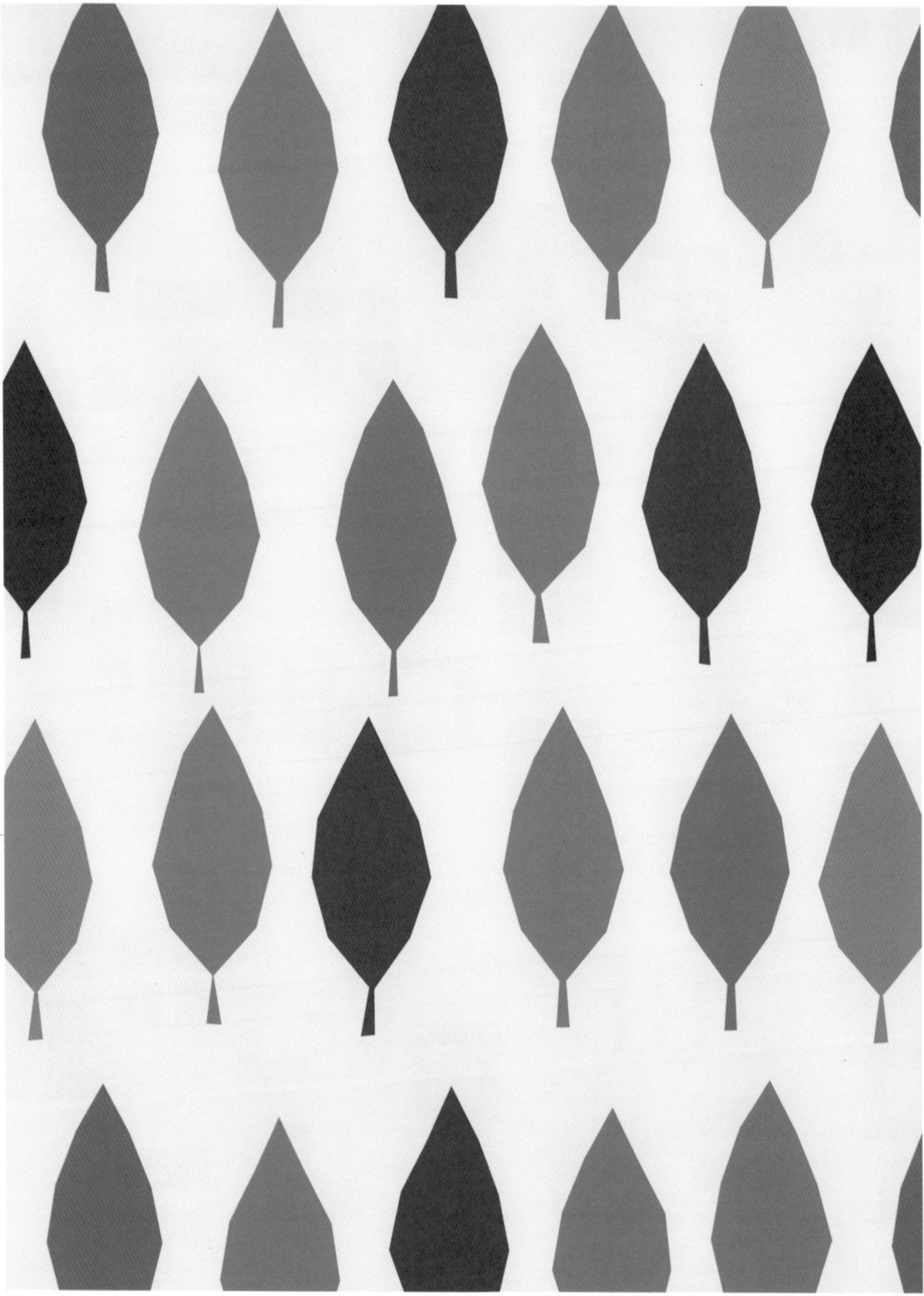

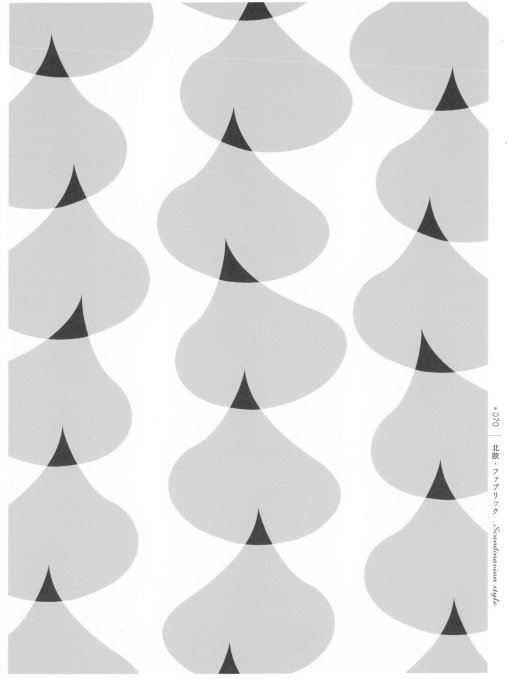

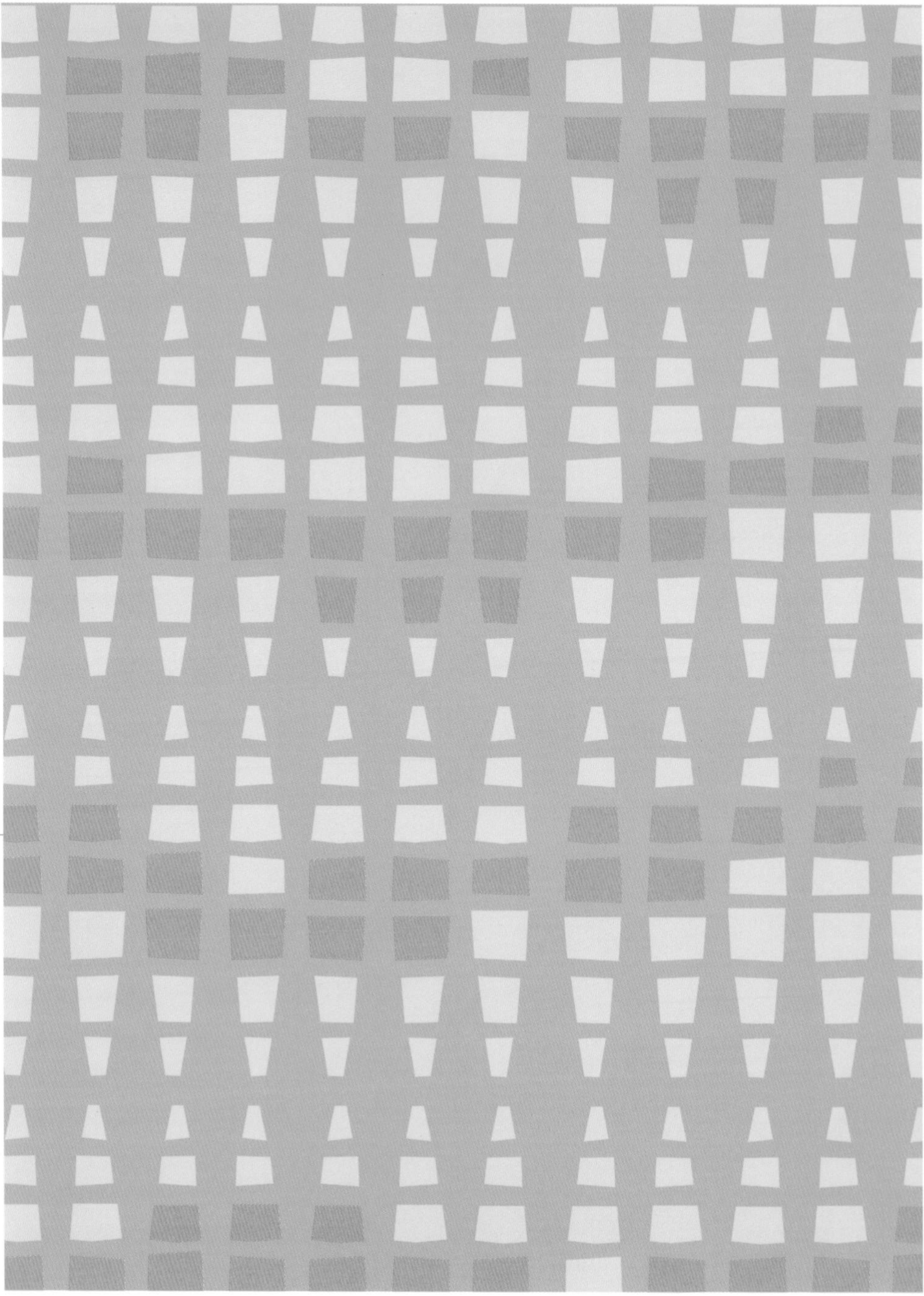

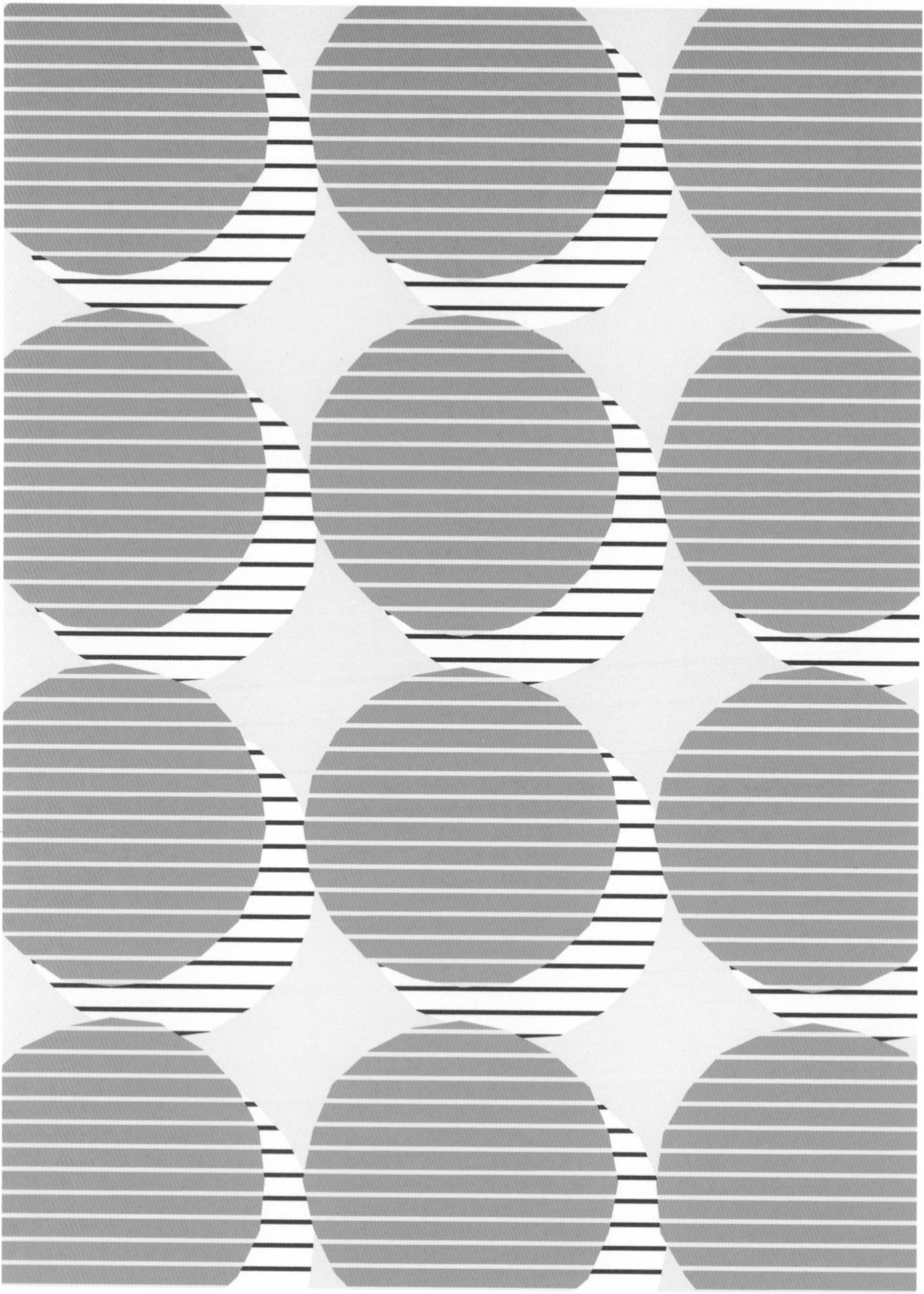

•073 北欧・ファブリック *Scandinavian style*

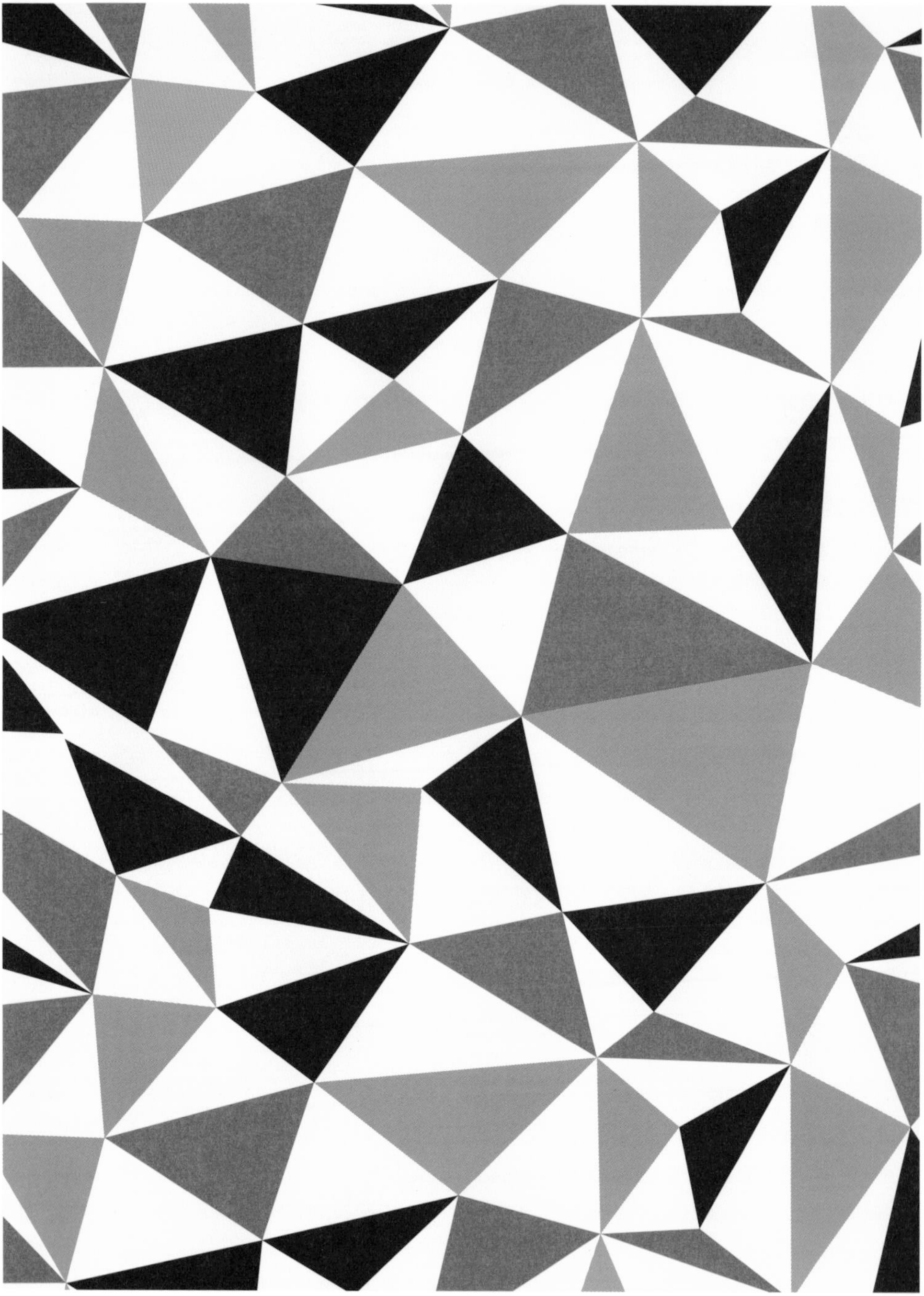

•075 | 北欧・ファブリック *Scandinavian style*

北欧・ファブリック　*Scandinavian style*

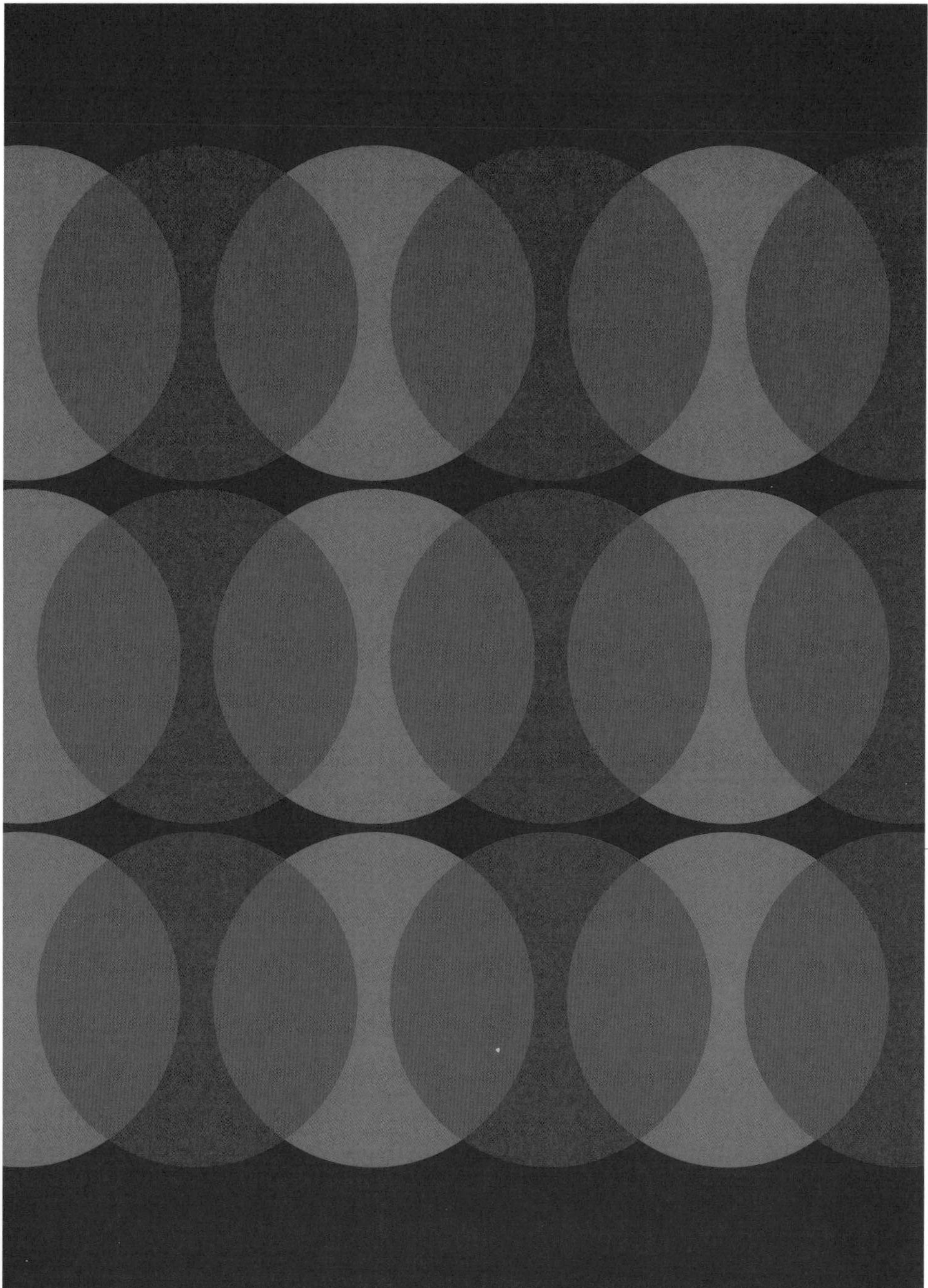

•084 北欧・ファブリック *Scandinavian style*

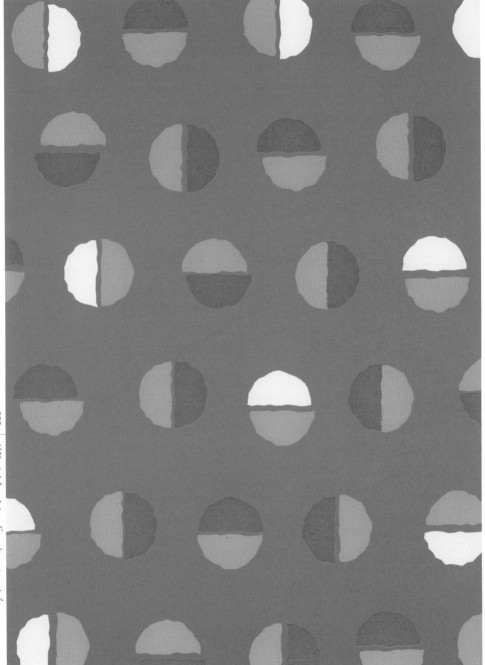

● 085

北欧・ファブリック *Scandinavian style*

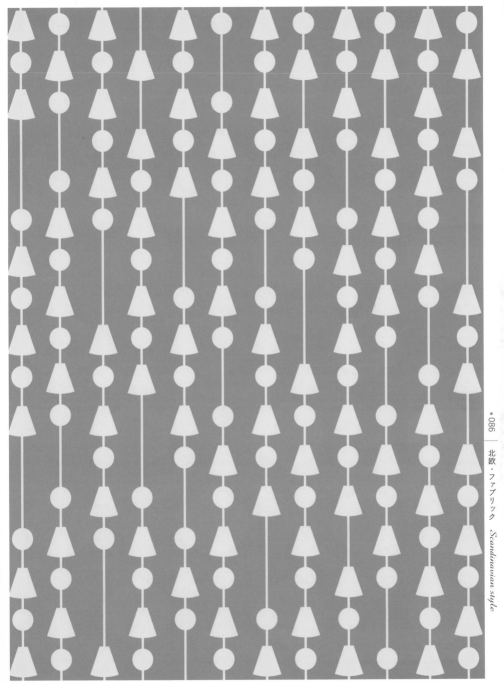

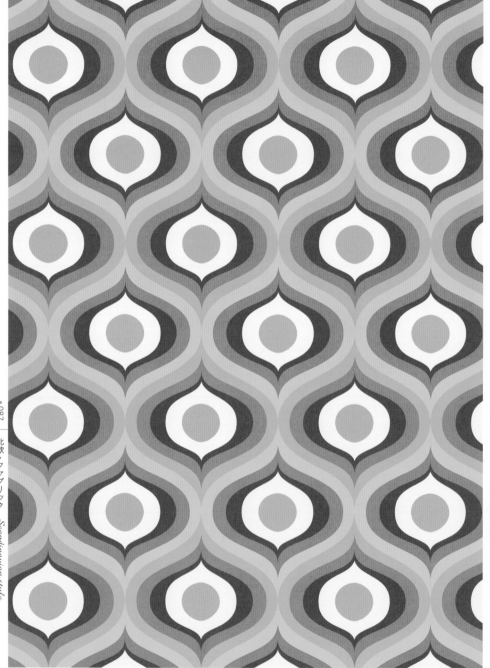

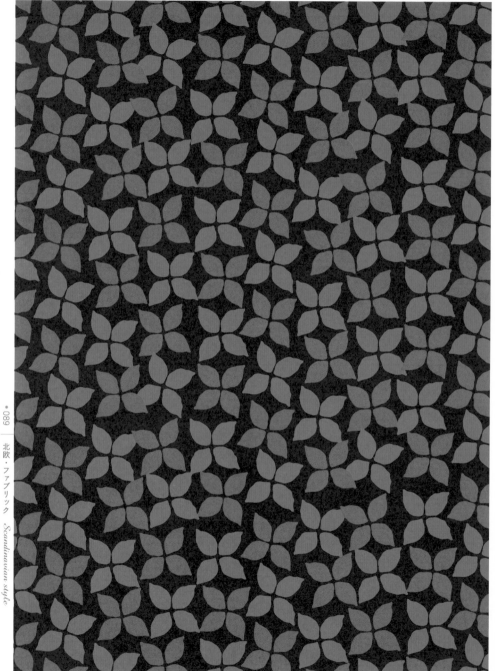

最
•090 ｜ 北欧・ファブリック *Scandinavian style*

・091 ｜ 北欧・ファブリック　*Scandinavian style*

092｜北欧・ファブリック Scandinavian style

北欧・ファブリック Scandinavian style

* 099

北欧・ファブリック　*Scandinavian style*

• 101　北欧・ファブリック　*Scandinavian style*

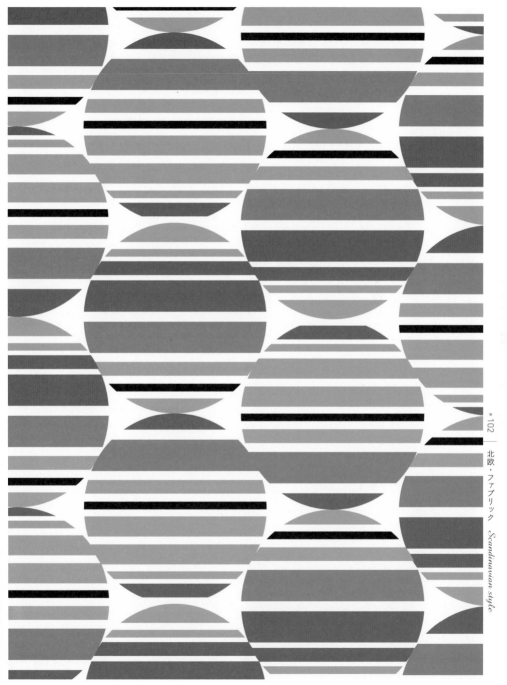

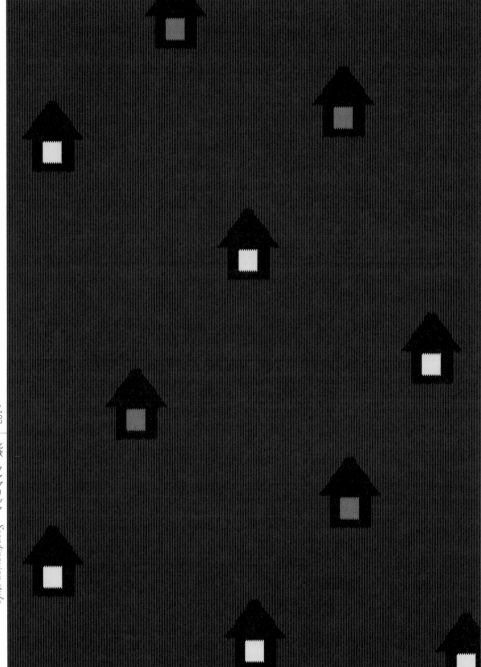

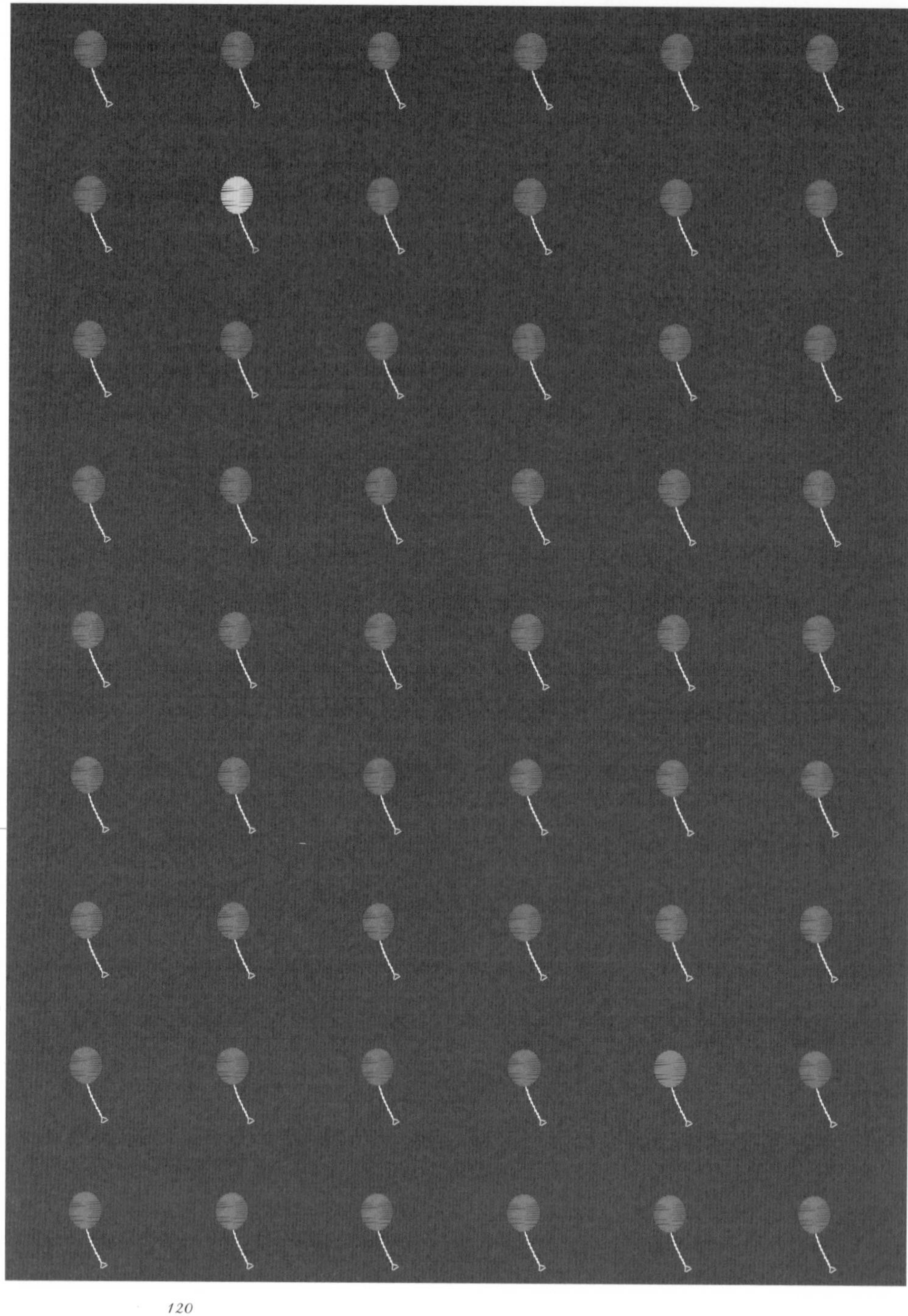

北欧・ファブリック　*Scandinavian style*

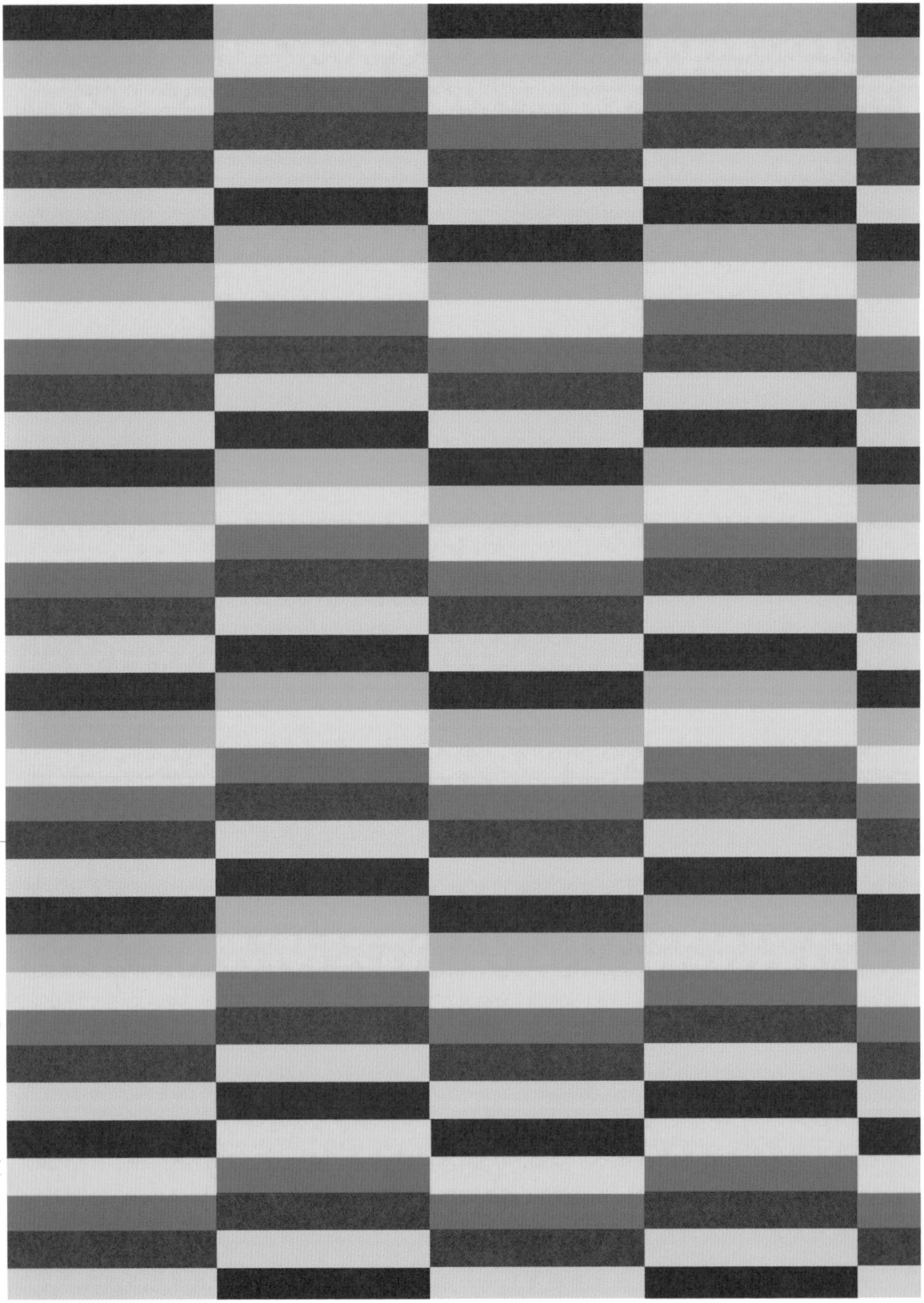

• 107 北欧・ファブリック *Scandinavian style*

北欧・ファブリック　*Scandinavian style*

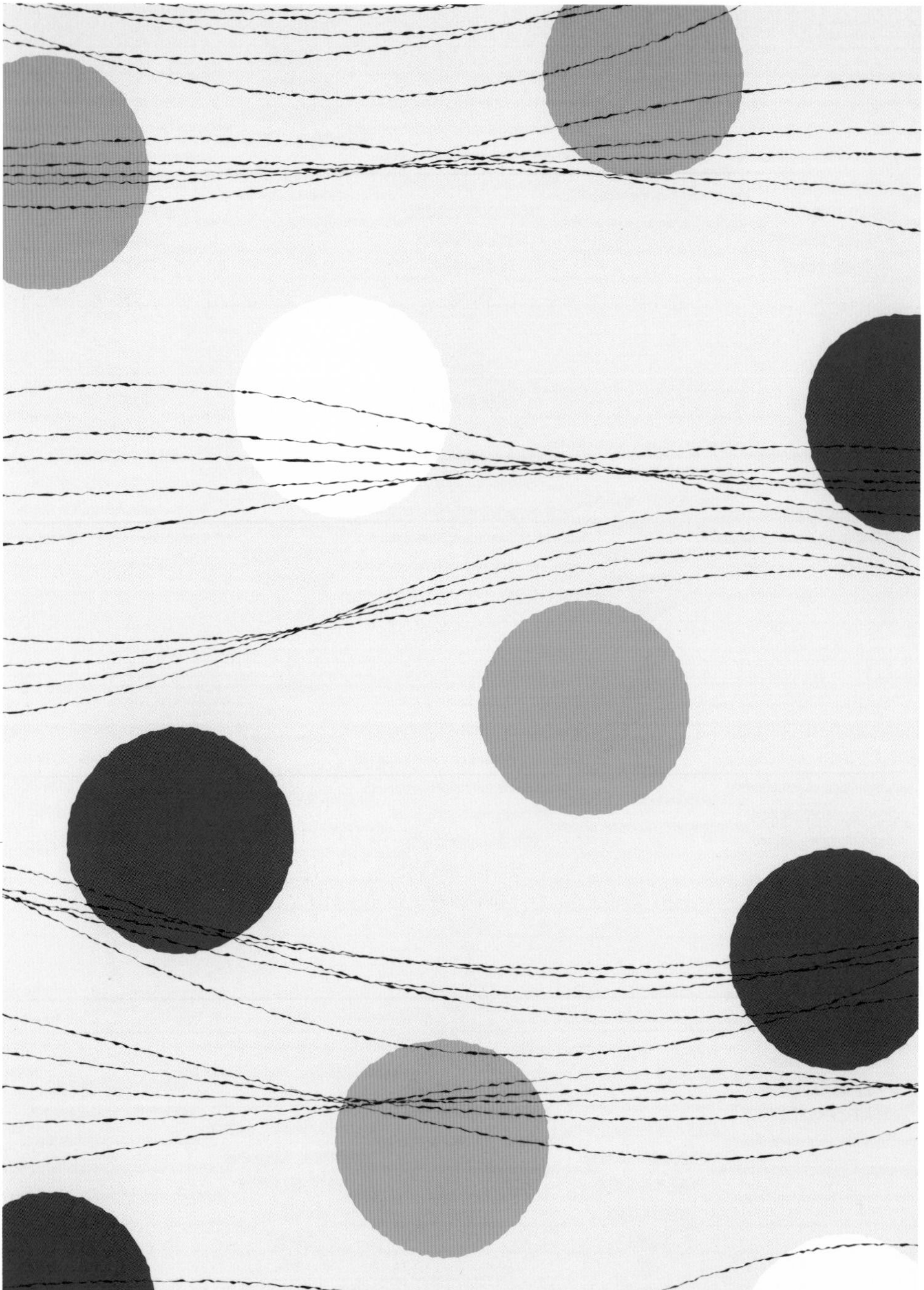

• 111 | 北欧・ファブリック *Scandinavian style*

北欧・ファブリック Scandinavian style

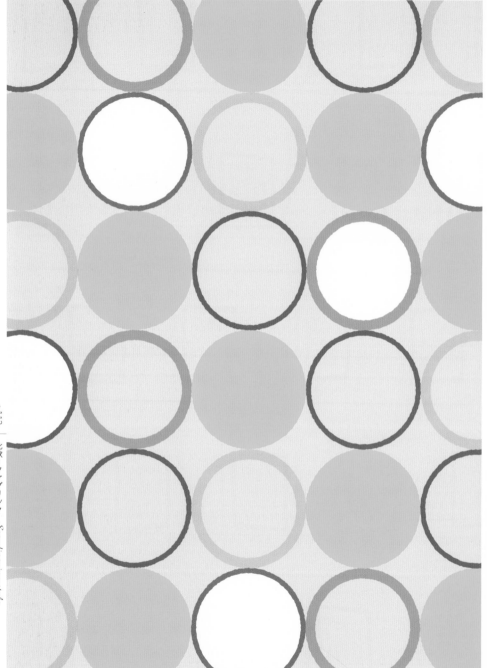

• 115 ｜ 北欧・ファブリック *Scandinavian style*

119 ・

北欧・ファブリック *Scandinavian style*

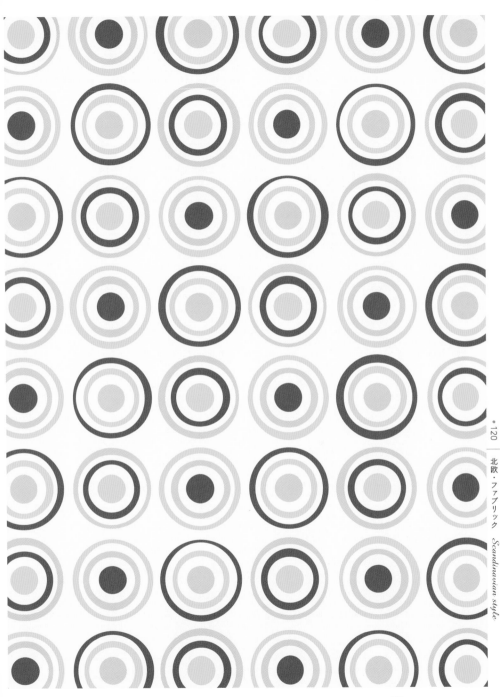

121 北欧・ファブリック Scandinavian style

北欧・ファブリック　Scandinavian style.

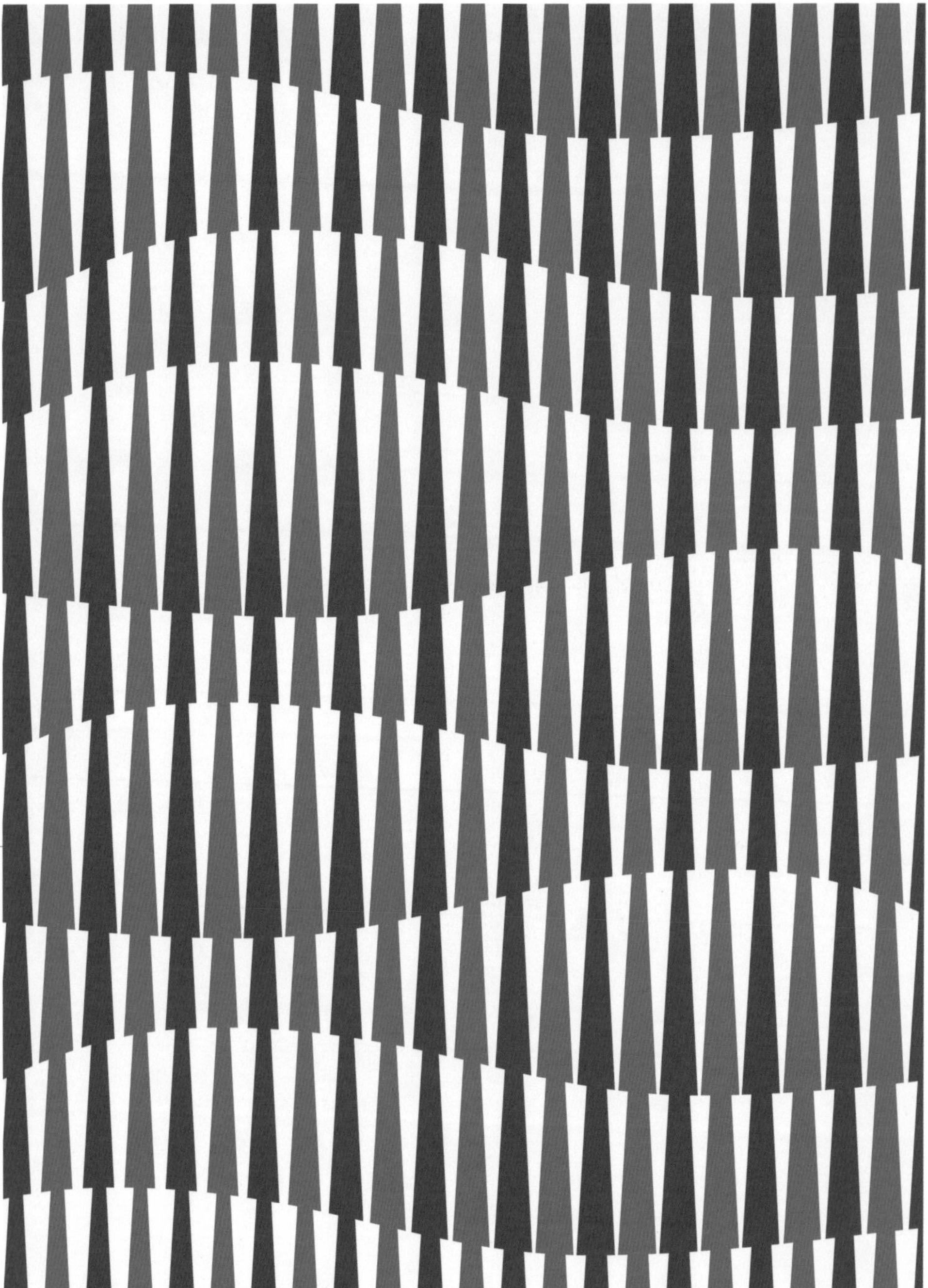

•125 北欧・ファブリック *Scandinavian style*

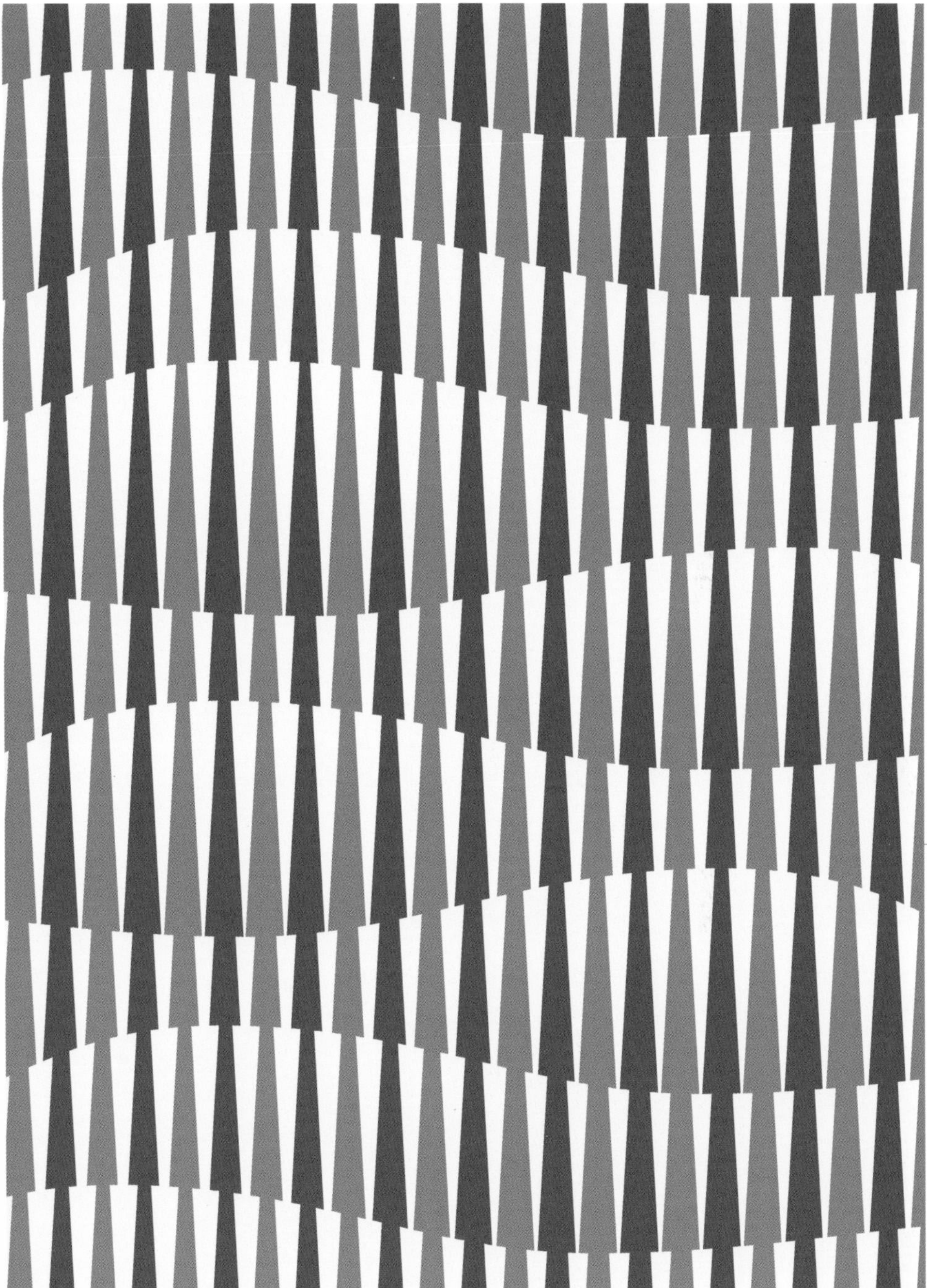

• 126

北欧・ファブリック *Scandinavian style*

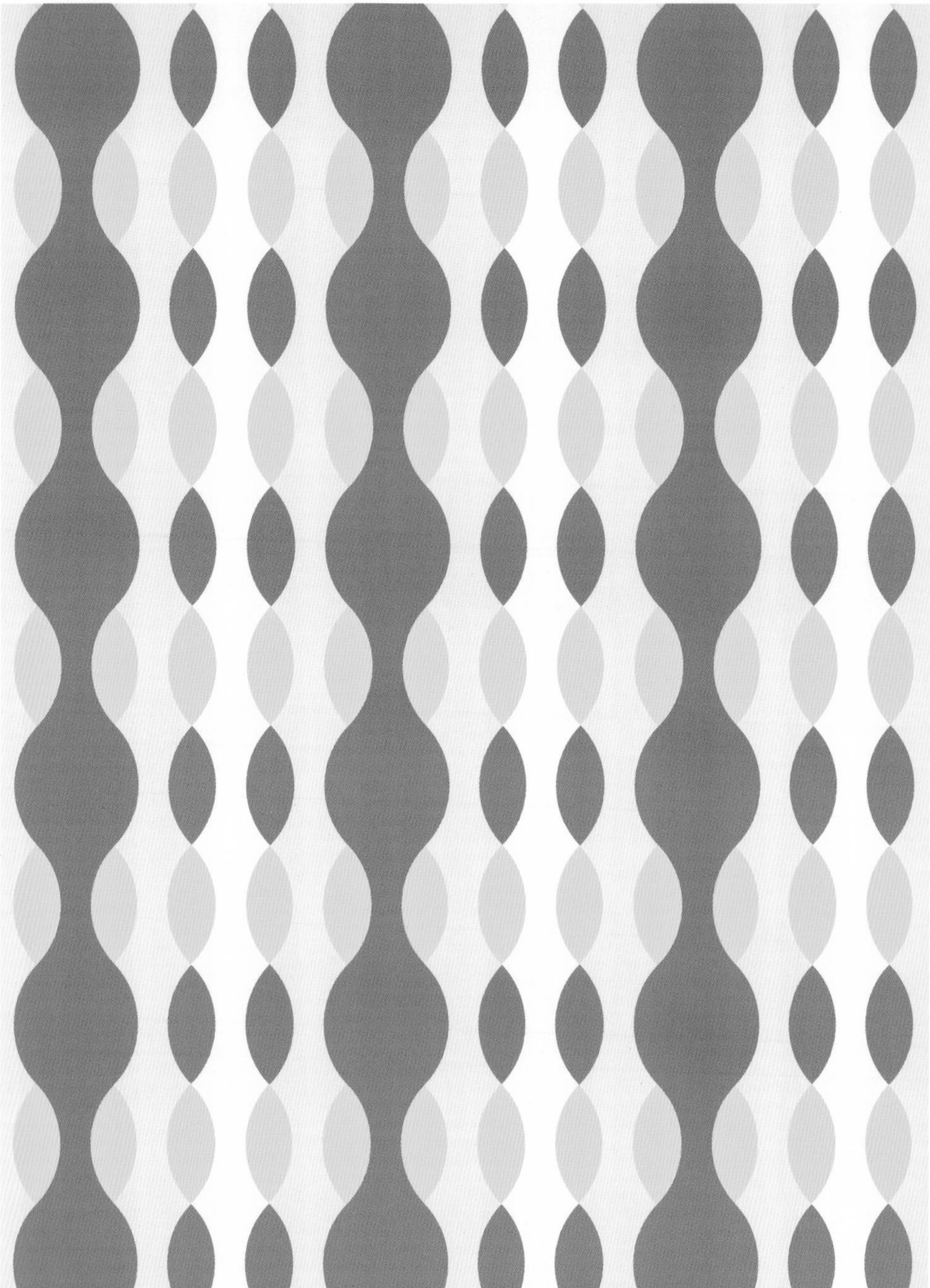

・127 北欧・ファブリック *Scandinavian style*

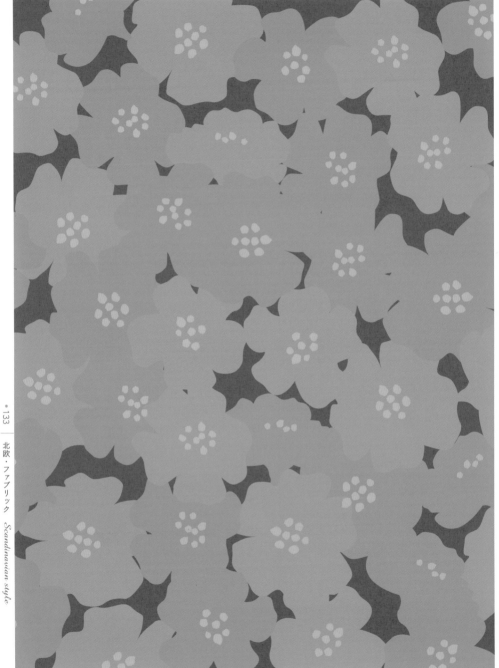

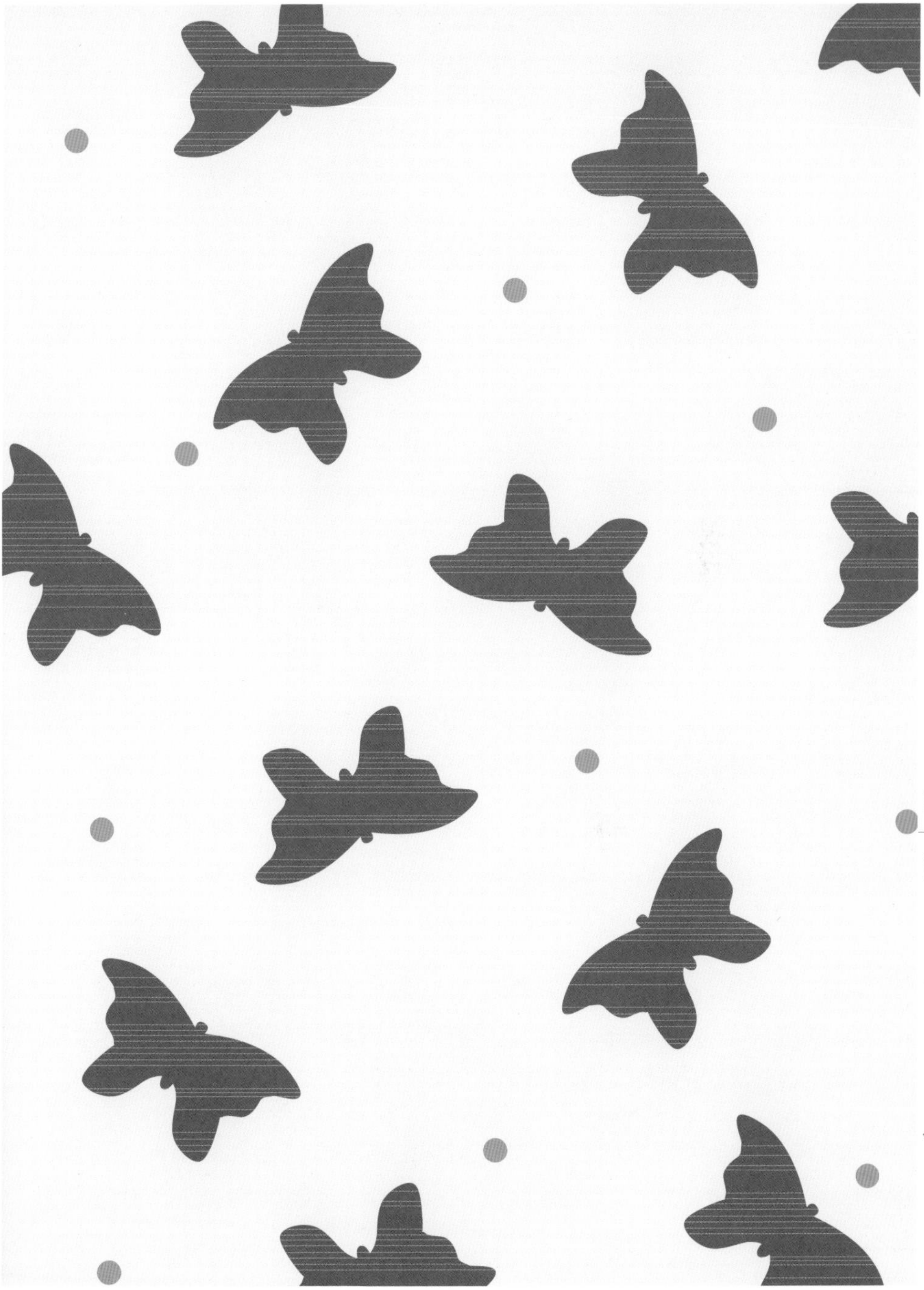

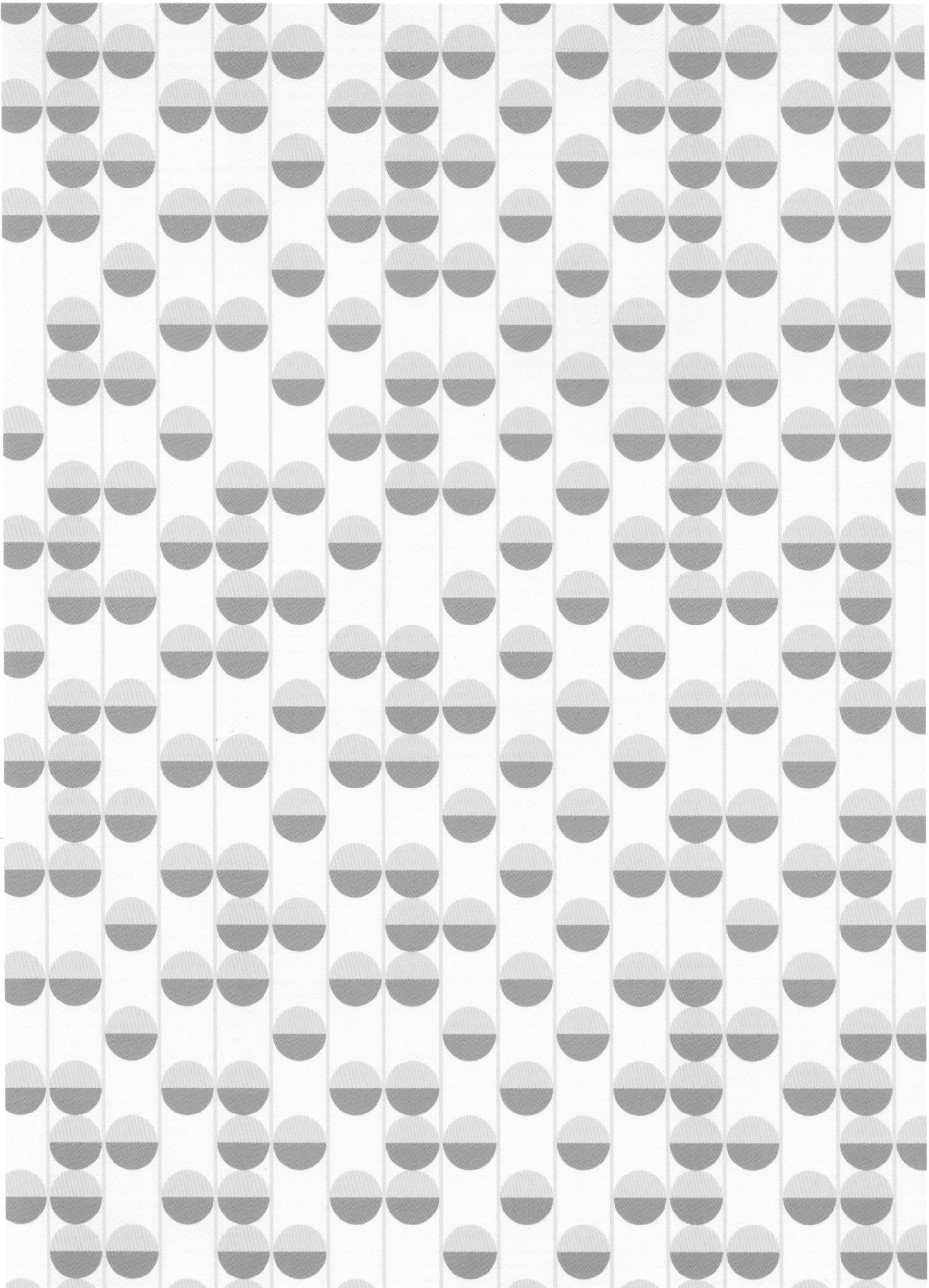

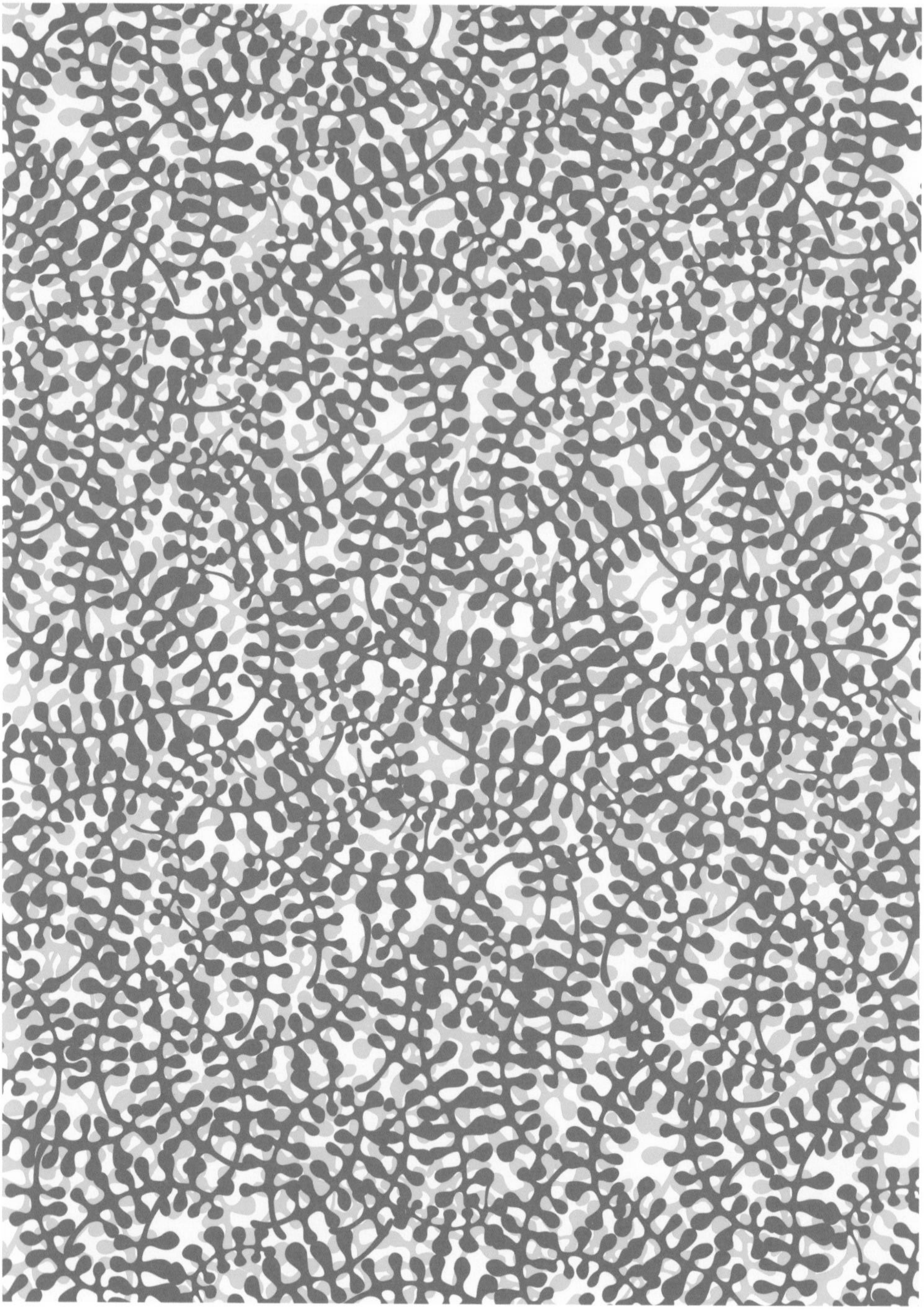

パターンの使い方

(Photoshop & Illustrator)

Petit Pattern Book

how to use patterns

はじめる前に

○注意すること

● CD-ROMをご使用になる前に、必ずP.175の使用許諾をお読みください。

● 本書では、Mac OS X（10.4.5）、Adobe Photoshop CS2、Adobe Illustrator CS2を用いて解説しています。
Windows XP Professional SP1でも動作確認済みですが、環境が異なる場合や、操作方法が分からないときは、
OSやソフトウェアに則した、お手持ちの説明書をお読みください。

● 「パターンをつかってつくるもの」（P.164-169）では、Illustratorとプリンタを使用します。

○準備

まずはCD-ROMをセットして、「Scandinavian-style」フォルダを開きます。必要なデータをピックアップしてデスクトップにコピーしましょう。
「Scandinavian-style」フォルダを開くと、「JPEG」と「EPS」と「Template」という3つのフォルダが入っています。「Template」フォルダに入っているデータは、P.164以降で使うサンプルデータです。

Mac

Win

○データの種類

掲載したすべてのパターンには、それぞれJPEGとEPSの2つの形式でファイルを用意しています。
（EPSファイルは、Illustratorのバージョン8.0で保存しています）

JPEG

EPS

*JPEGファイルとして収録したのは、350dpi（商業印刷に耐え得る解像度）に設定したときに、ほぼA5サイズの印刷面積を持つビットマップ画像。「Adobe Photoshop」をはじめとするビットマップ系のソフトウェアで編集できるほか、多くのソフトウェアで扱うことが可能です。

*EPSファイルとして収録したのは、拡大縮小を行っても画質が劣化しない、ベクトル画像。ドロー系のソフトウェア「Adobe Illustrator」でファイルを開くと、自在にカスタマイズできます（ビットマップ系のソフトウェア「Adobe Photoshop」で開くと、「ラスタライズ」という工程を経て、ビットマップイメージに展開します）。

パターンで塗る

tiling

収録したファイルは、どれもタイリング(タイルのように敷き詰めること)が可能な、パターン(繰り返し模様)になっています。PhotoshopやIllustratorといったグラフィックソフトウェアで、パターンを登録する機能を使うと、繰り返し模様を一瞬にして好きなだけ、タイリングできます。いずれのソフトウェアでも「塗り」の設定を用いることから、本書ではこれを「パターンで塗る」と呼びます。

パターンで塗るのは初めて、という人に向けて、ここではPhotoshopとIllustratorを用いて、その設定方法を中心に説明していきます。

○データを開く

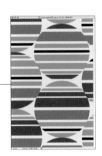

Photoshop

「ファイル」メニューから「開く」を選択し、パターンファイル(ここではJPEGファイル)を開きます。

Illustrator

「ファイル」メニューから「開く」を選択し、パターンファイル(ここではEPSファイル)を開きます。選んだパターンがページ中央に表れます。

パターンで塗る
tiling

「Photoshop」編

1. パターンを登録する

好きなパターンファイルを選んでPhotoshopで開き
ます。「選択範囲」メニューから「すべてを選択」を選ん
でパターン全体を選択し、「編集」メニューから「パター
ン定義」を選びます。パターンをいつでも使えるように、
分かりやすい名前をつけておきます。

2. 登録したパターンを選ぶ

「ファイル」メニューから「新規」を選んで、パターンで塗
りたい空白の画像ファイルを作成します。ツールバーの
塗りつぶしツールをダブルクリックし、オプションで「パタ
ーン」を選ぶと、先ほど定義したパターンが選択できる
ようになります。

3. パターンで塗る

塗りつぶしツールで画像上の適当な箇所をクリックして、
パターンで塗りつぶします。

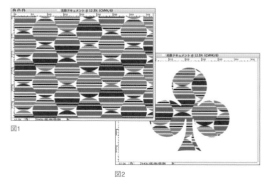

図1

図2

＊図1は、A3サイズの空白のファイル
を塗りつぶしたものです。図2のよう
にあらかじめ選択ツールで塗りつぶ
す範囲や形を選択しておくと、パター
ンで選択範囲内のみを塗りつぶすこ
とができます。

パターンで塗る
tiling

「Illustrator」編

1. パターンを登録する

好きなパターンファイルを選んでIllustratorで開きます。「選択」メニューから「すべてを選択」でパターン全体を選択し、「編集」メニューから「コピー」を選ぶとパターンがコピーされます。

「ファイル」メニューから「新規」で空白のドキュメントを作成し、「編集」メニューから「ペースト」を選んでパターンをペーストします。パターン全体が選択された状態のまま、「編集」→「パターン設定」を選んで新規スウォッチを作成し、パターンをいつでも使えるように、分かりやすい名前をつけておきます。

2. 登録したパターンを選ぶ

登録が終わったら、ペーストしたパターンが必要なくなるので、パターン全体が選択された状態のまま、「編集」メニューから「消去」を選んで消します。

「ウインドウ」メニューから「スウォッチ」を選び、スウォッチパレットを表示します。スウォッチパレット内に新たに作成したパターンスウォッチが登録されているので、クリックします。

3. パターンで塗る

パターンで塗るオブジェクトを作成します。

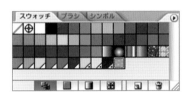

図1

図2

＊図1は、長方形ツールで四角形を描いたものです。図2のように他のドローツールで、パターンで塗りつぶされた複雑なオブジェクトを描くこともできます。

番外編 1

「Illustrator」をつかってパターンの色を変える

Step ❶

IllustratorでEPSファイルを開き、「ウインドウ」メニューから「スウォッチ」を選択して、スウォッチパレットを表示します。続いて、変更したい色のスウォッチをダブルクリックして、「スウォッチオプション」を表示します。

＊収録されたEPSファイルのほとんどは、色や形ごとにレイヤー分けされています。それぞれのレイヤーの順番を入れ替えたり、非表示にしたり、いろいろなアレンジが可能になっています。

Step ❷

「スウォッチオプション」上にあるカラーパレットでCMYKを好きな色に変更します。その際「プレビュー」にチェックを入れておくと、色がパターンにすぐに反映されるので便利です。色が決定したら「OK」をクリックします。

＊Illustratorで開いたEPSファイルは、サイズを変えたり、形を変えたり、要素を足したり引いたりと、自由自在。でも、加工したパターンをスウォッチに登録して使いたい場合は、タイリングで繋がる部分の四辺のアートワークを、加工で崩してしまわないよう気を付けましょう。

Step ❸

1〜2を繰り返して、オリジナルパターンの出来上がり。別名で保存しておきましょう。

＊Photoshopで開いたJPEGファイルの色を変更することも可能ですが、複雑な輪郭で描かれたパターンは、塗りつぶしツールできれいに色を変更できないことがあります。そういった場合には、「イメージ」メニューから「色調補正」→「カラーバランス」もしくは「色相・彩度」で色味を調整することができます。同じパターンのEPSファイルをまずはIllustratorで開いて色を変更し、別名でJPEG保存したものを、次にPhotoshopで開いて使う方法もあります。

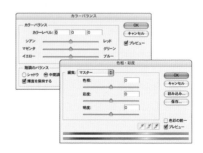

番外編 2

パターンをデスクトップの壁紙にする

Step 1

Photoshopで壁紙に設定したいパターンのJPEGファイルを開いて、「イメージ」メニューから「画像解像度」を選択し、モニタ表示に充分な「72dpi」に解像度を設定し直して、別名で保存します。

Step 2

- for Mac -

Macでは、「アップル」メニューから「システム環境設定」→「デスクトップとスクリーンセーバ」を選択します。「フォルダを選択」から先ほど別名で保存したファイルを指定し、「タイル状に配置」にすると、デスクトップにパターンが表示されます。

- for Win -

Windowsでは、「コントロールパネル」で「画面」を選択し、「画面のプロパティ」を開きます(デスクトップ上で右クリックして選択することもできます)。「デスクトップ」から先ほど別名で保存したファイルを指定し、「並べて表示」にすると、デスクトップにパターンが表示されます。

and more !

パターンをウェブサイトの背景にする

上のStep 1で「72dpi」に解像度を設定し直したデータは、ホームページの背景にも使えます。
この際にはJPEGファイルを、写真以外のアートワークの保存に適した、GIF形式に置き換えることをおすすめします。

ピンクッションをつくる

パターンを使ってナチュラルでふんわりやさしい
オリジナルのピンクッションを。チクチク針仕事のときは
もちろん、お部屋のインテリアとしても活躍します。

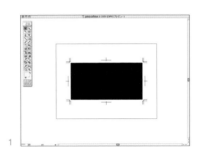

1

○用意するもの

専用布用紙、手芸用わた、ミシン、縫い針、糸、まち
針、はさみ

※専用布用紙はいくつかのメーカーからいろいろなタイプの商品が
出ています。使用するプリンタの機種・性能に合ったものを選びま
しょう。今回は裏側にPETフィルムが貼られていてインクジェット
プリンタで印刷できる、コットン製タイプのものを使用します。

1. 台紙データを開く

付属CD-ROMの「Template」フォルダの中にあ
る「pincushion.eps」をデスクトップにコピーし、
Illustratorで開きます。

2. パターンを使ってデザインする

次に、使いたいパターンを「スウォッチ」に登録しま
す（P.161参照）。

台紙データにはあらかじめトンボ（トリムマーク）
がついています。トンボはカットや折り目をつける
際に、目印となるものです。

仕上がりを想定しながら、パターンを使って自由
にデザインしてみましょう。

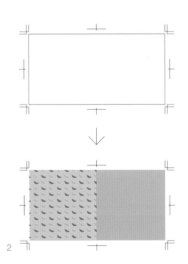

2

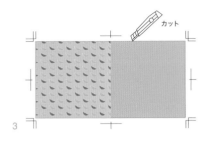

カット

3

3. 専用布用紙にプリントしてカットする

プリンタに専用布用紙をセットしてプリントします。今回使用している用紙は裏面にPETフィルムが貼られたタイプのものですが、同じように用紙には表裏があるので注意してセットしましょう(プリントの際の細かな設定は、各製品に記載されている注意事項に従って設定してください)。

プリントが終わったら、周りの不要な部分をカットし、裏に貼られているPETフィルムをはがします。

4. 縫製する

次に、四方にそれぞれ縫いしろを5mmずつとります。裏返しになるように半分に折って、3辺をミシンで縫います。残りの1辺は返し口として縫わずに開けておきます。

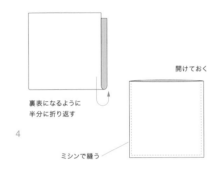

開けておく

裏表になるように
半分に折り返す

4

ミシンで縫う

5. わたをつめる

縫い合わせが終わったら裏返し、返し口からわたを詰めます。

6. 返し口を閉じる

わたを詰め終わったら、返し口を閉じます。

5

出来上がり!

仕上げにレースリボンをあしらったり、端にループを縫いとめて、ひっかけられるようにしたり。こんなふうに重ねてディスプレイするときは、わたにほんの少しのポプリを混ぜてもよいですね。

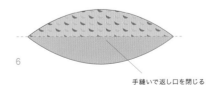

6

手縫いで返し口を閉じる

ファブリックパネルをつくる

雑貨屋さんなどで売っているファブリックパネルは、
意外と高価で手の出しにくいものです。お気に入りのパターンを
使って自分で作ると案外簡単。愛着も湧きますね。

1

○ヨコのサイズ = (a) + (c) ×2 + 約40mm(折り返し部分)
○タテのサイズ = (b) + (c) ×2 + 約40mm(折り返し部分)
※パネルのサイズに合わせて適宜調整してください。

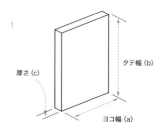

2

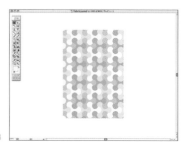

3

○用意するもの

木製パネル(画材店などで入手できます)、専用布
用紙、白い布、ガンタッカー(なければ画びょうで
も可)、壁掛け用金具(吊カン)、ひも、定規、ハサミ、
ドライバー

1. サイズを決める

木製パネルのヨコ幅(a)、タテ幅(b)、厚さ(c)を定規
で測ります。次に、それらに折り返し部分となる約
40mm(約20mm×2)を加えて、作成するファブ
リックのサイズを決定します。

2. データの準備をする

1で決定したサイズの長方形オブジェクトをIllustrator
で作成します。長方形ツールを選択し、optionキー
(WindowsはAltキー)を押しながら画面をクリッ
クすると、数値で長方形の幅と高さを設定できま
す。1で決定したサイズを入力しましょう。

3. パターンで塗る

次に、使いたいパターンを「スウォッチ」に登録しま
す(P.161参照)。選択ツールを選び、2で作成し
た長方形を選択し、オブジェクトの塗りに先ほど
登録したパターンを設定します。これでデータの
出来上がりです。

4. 専用布用紙にプリントしてカットする

プリンタに専用布用紙をセットしてプリントします。今回使用している用紙は裏面にPETフィルムが貼られたタイプのものですが、同じように用紙には表裏があるので注意してセットしましょう（プリントの際の細かな設定は、各製品に記載されている注意事項に従って設定してください）。

プリントが終わったら、周りの不要な部分をカットし、裏に貼られているPETフィルムをはがします。

5. 木製パネルの準備

ファブリックを直接木製パネルに貼ると地が透けてしまうので、あらかじめ下地として白い布を貼っておきます。1で決定したファブリックのサイズと同じ大きさの白い布を用意し、ガンタッカー（なければ画びょうでも可）を使って木製パネルに貼っていきます。片側を先にとめて、生地を引っぱりながらもう一方をとめるのがコツです。角の部分は余った布を折りたたむようにすると、きれいに仕上がります。

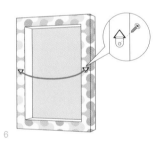

6. ファブリックを木製パネルに貼る

4でプリントしたファブリックを5と同じ要領で下地の上に貼っていきます。

次に、パネルの裏側に壁掛け用の金具（吊カン）を取り付けます。おおよその位置を決め、吊カンをドライバーで固定し、ひもを通して完成です。

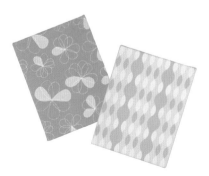

出来上がり！

いくつか作って並べると、味わいのあるすてきな空間に。デスク周りや壁に飾れば、ふと目を休ませてくれる、心地よいオブジェになります。

オリジナルエコバッグをつくる

パターンをアクセントにしてお手製のエコバッグを。
お買い物のときはもちろん、お弁当を入れたりとなにかと便利。
ゴミの減量にもなって環境にもやさしいですね。

※アイロンプリント専用紙は、お手持ちのプリンタのメーカーが製造する純正のアイロンプリントペーパーを使用するか、いくつかのメーカーから発売されている専用紙を購入して使用します（「インクジェット専用」などプリンタの種類に合わせて選びましょう）。用紙サイズはデザインに合わせて決めます。アイロンは家庭用アイロンで180〜200℃の温度が出れば問題ありません。

○用意するもの

エコバッグ、アイロンプリント専用紙、アイロン、アイロン台、はさみ

1. パターンを使ってデザインする

まずは、使いたいパターンを「スウォッチ」に登録します（P.161参照）。次にパスで作ったオブジェクトの塗りに、スウォッチに登録したパターンを設定します。デザインは自由に。文字を入れるのもよいでしょう。

2. 試しに普通の紙にプリントする

アイロンプリント専用紙にプリントする前に、普通紙にプリントします。実際に切り抜いてエコバッグに合わせ、仕上がりのサイズや位置を確認しましょう。イメージに合うまでこの作業を何度か繰り返し、デザインを決めます。

✂ カット

SAVE
THE
EARTH

1-2

3

3. アイロンプリント専用紙にプリントする

デザインが完成したら、アイロンプリント専用紙にプリントしましょう。まず表裏を確認し、用紙をプリンタにセットします。印刷設定画面で用紙の種類を「アイロンプリント用紙」に設定し、プリントを開始します（※アイロンプリントは左右反転されて印刷されます。用紙の種類に「アイロンプリント用紙」がない場合は、あらかじめ画像を左右反転しておきましょう）。

4

4. カットする

印刷が終わったら、アイロンプリント用紙の余白部分をはさみでカットします。転写部分から5mm程度の余白を残してカットすると、仕上がりがきれいになります。

5-7

5. アイロン台を準備する

アイロン台はなるべく硬めのものがよいでしょう。用意できない場合は、硬くて平らで耐熱性のある机の上に新聞を15〜20枚ほど敷き、その上に転写部分より大きい普通紙か布をかぶせて代用しましょう。

6. アイロンを熱くする

アイロンを熱くします。温度は「180〜200℃」に設定して「ドライ」の状態で充分加熱します（温度が低いと仕上がりがきれいにならない場合があります）。

8

7. 転写する

転写したい面を上にして、エコバッグをアイロン台に置きます。続いてその上に、先ほど切り抜いたアイロンプリント用紙を配置します。最初に軽く全体をアイロンがけして位置を固定させてから、強めにしっかりとアイロンをかけます。押し付ける力が弱いと充分に転写されず、はがれやすくなるので体重をかけて念入りに行いましょう。

8. アイロンプリント用紙をはがす

アイロンをかけた直後は温度が高くなっているので、充分に温度が冷めるまで待ちます（2〜3分）。冷めたら端からアイロンプリント用紙をゆっくりとはがします。

出来上がり！

北欧・ファブリック
Scandinavian style

おしゃれなパターン素材集
Petit Pattern Book

°001
scan-style001

°002
scan-style002

°003
scan-style003

°004
scan-style004

°005
scan-style005

°006
scan-style006

°007
scan-style007

°008
scan-style008

°009
scan-style009

°010
scan-style010

°011
scan-style011

°012
scan-style012

°013
scan-style013

°014
scan-style014

°015
scan-style015

°016
scan-style016

°017
scan-style017

°018
scan-style018

°019
scan-style019

°020
scan-style020

*021
scan-style021

*022
scan-style022

*023
scan-style023

*024
scan-style024

*025
scan-style025

*026
scan-style026

*027
scan-style027

*028
scan-style028

*029
scan-style029

*030
scan-style030

*031
scan-style031

*032
scan-style032

*033
scan-style033

*034
scan-style034

*035
scan-style035

*036
scan-style036

*037
scan-style037

*038
scan-style038

*039
scan-style039

*040
scan-style040

*041
scan-style041

*042
scan-style042

*043
scan-style043

*044
scan-style044

*045
scan-style045

*046
scan-style046

*047
scan-style047

*048
scan-style048

*049
scan-style049

*050
scan-style050

°051
scan-style051

°052
scan-style052

°053
scan-style053

°054
scan-style054

°055
scan-style055

°056
scan-style056

°057
scan-style057

°058
scan-style058

°059
scan-style059

°060
scan-style060

°061
scan-style061

°062
scan-style062

°063
scan-style063

°064
scan-style064

°065
scan-style065

°066
scan-style066

°067
scan-style067

°068
scan-style068

°069
scan-style069

°070
scan-style070

°071
scan-style071

°072
scan-style072

°073
scan-style073

°074
scan-style074

°075
scan-style075

°076
scan-style076

°077
scan-style077

°078
scan-style078

°079
scan-style079

°080
scan-style080

°081
scan-style081

°082
scan-style082

°083
scan-style083

°084
scan-style084

°085
scan-style085

°086
scan-style086

°087
scan-style087

°088
scan-style088

°089
scan-style089

°090
scan-style090

°091
scan-style091

°092
scan-style092

°093
scan-style093

°094
scan-style094

°095
scan-style095

°096
scan-style096

°097
scan-style097

°098
scan-style098

°099
scan-style099

°100
scan-style100

°101
scan-style101

°102
scan-style102

°103
scan-style103

°104
scan-style104

°105
scan-style105

°106
scan-style106

°107
scan-style107

°108
scan-style108

°109
scan-style109

°110
scan-style110

°111
scan-style111

°112
scan-style112

°113
scan-style113

°114
scan-style114

°115
scan-style115

°116
scan-style116

°117
scan-style117

°118
scan-style118

°119
scan-style119

°120
scan-style120

°121
scan-style121

°122
scan-style122

°123
scan-style123

°124
scan-style124

°125
scan-style125

°126
scan-style126

°127
scan-style127

°128
scan-style128

°129
scan-style129

°130
scan-style130

°131
scan-style131

°132
scan-style132

°133
scan-style133

°134
scan-style134

°135
scan-style135

°136
scan-style136

°137
scan-style137

°138
scan-style138

°139
scan-style139

°140
scan-style140

『おしゃれなパターン素材集　北欧・ファブリック』
付属CD-ROM使用許諾書（ソフトウェアライセンス契約書）

1. ライセンス

1) 株式会社ビー・エヌ・エヌ新社（以下「弊社」という。）は、本製品を購入され、本使用許諾書記載の条件に
合意されたお客様（以下「ユーザー」という。）に対し、本ソフトウェアを同時に1台のコンピュータ上でのみ
使用できる、譲渡不能の非独占的権利を許諾します。

2) ユーザーは、2の「制限事由」に該当する場合を除き、本ソフトウェアに含まれる素材を加工・編集し、もしく
は他の素材と組み合わせるなどして、主に以下のデザインに使用することができます。
　○ WEBなどのデジタルメディア
　○ 店舗の内装、案内表示などのグラフィックツール
　○ 印刷物として頒布するチラシ、フライヤー、ポスター、DM、カタログ、パンフレットなどの広告・販売促進ツール
　○ 個人制作・個人利用の雑貨、服、グリーティングカード、名刺など
　　（個人的・職業的・商業的用途の利用を認めますが、いずれも非売品のデザインに限ります。個人においても
　　素材を利用した制作物の販売は行えません。次の制限事由をよくお読み下さい。）

2. 制限事由

以下の行為を禁止します。

1) 本ソフトウェアを1台のコンピュータで使用するためのやむを得ぬ場合を除き、本ソフトウェアを複製すること

2) 本使用許諾書に基づくライセンスを他に譲渡し、本製品の貸与もしくはその他の方法で本ソフトウェアを他者
に使用させること

3) 流通を目的とした商品のデザインに素材を利用すること

4) 素材を利用してポストカード、名刺、雑貨などの制作販売または制作サービスを行うこと

5) 素材を利用してインターネットによるダウンロードサービスを行うこと（グリーティングカード・サービスを含む。）

6) 素材をホームページ上で公開する場合に、オリジナルデータがダウンロード可能となる環境を作ること

7) ソフトウェア製品等を製造・販売するために素材を流用すること

8) 素材そのものや素材を用いた制作物について意匠権などの権利を取得すること

9) 素材を公序良俗に反する目的、誹謗・中傷目的で利用すること

3. 著作権、その他の知的財産権

本ソフトウェアおよび素材に関する著作権、その他の知的財産権は、弊社または弊社への供給者の排他的財産として
留保されています。素材を利用した制作物においてユーザーの著作権を明示する場合は、併せてパターンの著作権
「©2006 2m09cmGRAPHICS, Inc.」を明示してください。

4. 責任の制限

弊社および弊社への供給者は、請求原因の如何を問わず、本ソフトウェアの使用または使用の不能および素
材の利用から生じるすべての損害や不利益（利益の逸失およびデータの損壊を含む。）につき、一切責任を負
わないものとします。

5. 使用許諾の終了

ユーザーが本使用許諾書に違反した場合、弊社は、本使用許諾書に基づくユーザーのライセンスを終了させる
ことができます。

Petit Pattern Book

How to use patterns
(Photoshop & Illustrator)

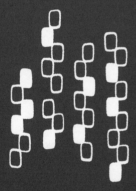

Before you start

○ Notes

- Please read the License Agreement on page 190 before you start.
- The explanation in this book is based on Mac OS X (10.4.5), Adobe Photoshop CS2, and Adobe Illustrator CS2. The functionality has also been verified with Windows XP Professional SP1. If your system is different, or if you have a question concerning the operation of the software, refer to the manuals corresponding to your OS and software.
- In the chapter "Let's use the patterns to make an original article" (p184-189), you will be using Illustrator and your printer.

○ Preparation

At first, set the attached CD-ROM and open "Scandinavian -style" folder. Pick up the patterns you need and copy them to your desktop.

Open the folder "Scandinavian-style" and you will find three folders: "JPEG", "EPS", and "Template". You are going to use the data inside "Template" from p184 as sample data later on.

Mac

○ Different kinds of data

All the patterns in the book are prepared in the following two formats:
(EPS files are saved with Illustrator 8.0.)

JPEG

EPS

※In the JPEG file, you will find bitmap images which are printed on the surface of around 148× 210mm at 350 dpi (the resolution suitable for commercial printing). You can edit them with Adobe Photoshop and other bitmap software, and you can use it with many other types of software.

※In the EPS file, you will find vector images, which do not deteriorate when you increase or reduce the size. Open the file with Adobe Illustrator or other drawing software, and you will be able to customize the images freely (When you open the file with bitmap software such as Adobe Photoshop, the image will be developed as a bitmap image after the process called rasterizing).

Tiling with a pattern

All the files are repeated patterns which can be tiled. Register patterns in Photoshop, Illustrator or other graphic software, and you can tile one of the repeated patterns in the blink of an eye.

For those people who have never tiled with patterns, we shall explain how to do it using Photoshop and Illustrator, focusing on the settings.

● Open the data

Photoshop

Select "Open" from the "File" menu, and open the pattern file (JPEG file here).

Illustrator

Select "Open" from the "File" menu, and open the pattern file (EPS file here). The pattern chosen will appear in the centre of the screen.

How to tile with

Photoshop

1. Save the pattern

Open your favorite pattern with Photoshop. Select the whole image by choosing "Select" → "All", and select "Edit" → "Define Pattern". Give the pattern an easily recognized name so that you can use it whenever you want.

2. Select the saved pattern

Select "File" → "New" and create a blank image file to be filled with the pattern. Double click on Paint Bucket Tool and select "Pattern" from the options, and you are able to choose the pattern you have already defined.

3. Tiling with the pattern

Click on the image with the Paint Bucket Tool and tile the whole image with the pattern.

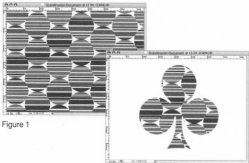

Figure 1

Figure 2

※Figure1 shows a blank 420× 297mm file tiled with a pattern. If you use Select tools to select the part of the image to be tiled, you can tile only the part and the shape you have selected.

How to tile with
Illustrator

1. Save the pattern

Open your favorite pattern with Illustrator. Select the whole image by choosing "Select"→"All", and "Edit"→"Copy" to copy the pattern.

Create a blank document by selecting "File"→"New", and paste the pattern by selecting "Edit"→"Paste". While the whole pattern is still selected, select "Edit"→"Define Pattern" to create a new swatch and give it an easily recognized name so that you can use it whenever you want.

2. Select the saved pattern

When you have saved the image, delete the pattern you pasted previously, as you do not need it any more. While the whole pattern is still selected, select "Edit"→"Clear" and the pattern will be deleted.

Select "Window"→"Swatches" to show the swatch pallet. Click the newly registered pattern on the swatch pallet.

3. Tiling with the pattern

Make an object to be tiled with the pattern.

Figure 1

Figure 2

※Figure 1 shows a rectangular shape drawn with the Rectangular Tool. You can also draw a complicated object tiled with the pattern with other tools, as shown in Figure 2.

Extra 1

How to change the color of a pattern with Illustrator

Step 1

Open the EPS file with Illustrator (see p179). Select "Window" → "Swatches" to show the swatch pallet. Double click the swatch of the color you would like to change to show "Swatch Options".

※Most of the EPS files have different layers for each color and shape: you can arrange the patterns by changing the layer orders or hiding a layer.

Step 2

Modify CMYK on the color pallet on "Swatch Options" to create your own color. You can select the "Preview" option beforehand to show the new color immediately. When you have obtained the color you want, click "OK".

※If you have opened the EPS file with Illustrator, you can modify the pattern any way you like: by changing the size, the shape, adding or taking out an element, etc. On the other hand, if you would like to save the modified pattern in Swatch for future use, avoid breaking the square artwork of its four sides, which would be juxtaposed on the tiling image.

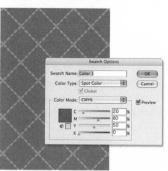

Step 3

Repeat 1-2 and create your own original pattern. Save it under a different name.

※While it is also possible to change the color of the JPEG file with Photoshop using the Paint Bucket Tool, the new color may be fuzzy in some patterns drawn using complicated lines. If this happens, select "Image" →"Adjustments"→"Color Balance" or "Hue/Saturation" to correct the color. Alternatively, open the EPS file of the same pattern with Illustrator, change the color, save as a JPEG file under a different name, and open and use it with Photoshop.

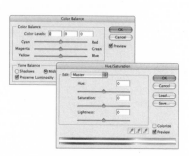

How to use the pattern as a desktop background of your computer

Step 1

Open the JPEG file with Photoshop (see p179), select "Image" → "Image Size". Change the resolution to "72 dpi", the resolution suitable for the monitor, and save it under a new name.

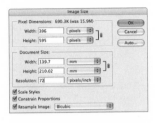

Step 2

-for Mac-

Go to the "Apple" menu and select "System Preferences" → "Desktop & Screen Saver". Select the saved file in Step1 for the desktop background, and choose "Tile" to make the pattern appear on the desktop.

-for Windows-

Go to "Control Panel", and open "Display Properties" (you can also select it by right-clicking your mouse on the desktop). Click the "Desktop" tab, select the saved file in Step1 for the background, and chose "Tile" to show the pattern on the desktop.

Using the pattern for the background of your website

The data at resolution "72 dpi" at Step1 above can also be used as the background of a website.
In this case, it is recommended that you transfer the date to the GIF format, which is suitable for saving artworks other than photos.

How to make a "pincushion"

Using the patterns, create an original pincushion, natural and soft to the touch, not only to make sewing more pleasant, but also as a stylish piece of decoration.

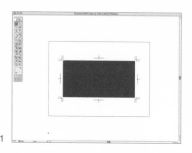

1

○ You will need:

Canvas cloth for use with a printer, padding cotton, a sewing machine, a sewing needle, sewing thread, marking pins and a pair of scissors

※ Various types of canvas cloth for printing are available from several manufacturers. Choose the one suitable for the type and functions of your printer. Here we are using cotton-lined canvas with PET film, which an Inkjet printer can print on.

1. Open the mount data

Find the "pincushion.eps" file in the "Template" folder in the attached CD-ROM. Copy it on to the desktop, and open it with Illustrator.

2. Design with patterns

Register the pattern you like in "Swatch" (see p181).

The mount in the CD-ROM is already marked with trimming lines, which serve as a guideline for creasing and cutting.

Feel free to use the patterns to create the design that pleases you most.

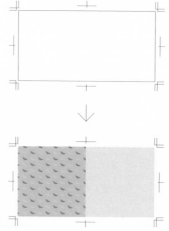

2

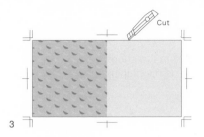

3

3. Print on the canvas cloth

Set the cloth in the printer and print the design out. Here, we're using canvas with a covering of PET film on the back. Watch out: all cloth for printing has a printing side (Stick to the detailed settings in the manual for the product you are using).

Cut off the blank part all round and peel off the PET film on the back.

4. Sew

Fold the cloth in two so that the printed surface is inside. Sew at 5mm from the border on the three sides. Leave the fourth side open to turn the cloth inside out.

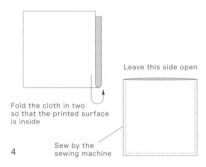

Leave this side open

Fold the cloth in two
so that the printed surface
is inside

4   Sew by the
sewing machine

5. Fill with the cotton

Turn the cloth inside out and fill the case with the cotton.

6. Close the cushion

Turn the cloth inside out and fill the case with the cotton.

5

Now your original pincushion is ready to use!

Decorate it with lace ribbons. Add a loop to hang it up with. If you pile them up as in the picture below, try adding a little of potpourri mixture with the padding.

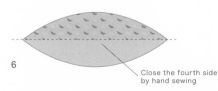

6   Close the fourth side
by hand sewing

How to make a "fabric wall plaque"

Fabric wall plaques are quite expensive to buy in the shops. Why not make one yourself – it is not as hard as might think, and you'll enjoy it as well.

1

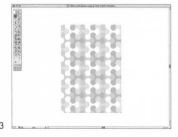

Thickness=(c)

Length=(b)

Width=(a)

○ Width of the canvas
=(a)+(c) × 2 + about 40mm (for the flaps)
○ Length of the canvas
=(b)+(c) × 2 + about 40mm (for the flaps)
※Please adjust according to the side of a panel.

2

3

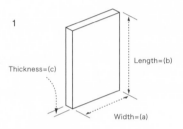

○ You will need:

A wooden panel (available at shops that sell drawing materials), canvas cloth for use with a printer, plain white cloth, a tucker gun (or drawing pins), D-hooks for hanging, string, a ruler, a pair of scissors and a screw driver

1. Calculate the size

Measure the width (a), the length (b), and the thickness (c) of your panel with a ruler. Add the size of the flaps, about 40mm (about 20mm × 2), to work out the size of the canvas.

2. Prepare the data

Make a rectangular object of which the size is calculated in advance: Choose the Rectangular tool, and click the top of the screen, at the same time holding down the "Option" key ("Alt" key for Windows), then, you can make a rectangular object of a size which you can determine. Input the size you decide on.

3. Tile with the pattern

Register the patterns you like in "Swatch" (see p181). Select the rectangle you've just made with the "Select" tool and select the patterns which you have saved to paint the rectangular. The data is now ready to be printed.

4

4. Print on the canvas cloth and cut

Set the cloth in the printer and print the design out. Here, we're using canvas with a covering of PET film on the back. Watch out: all cloth for printing has a printing side (Stick to the detailed settings in the manual for the product you are using).

Cut off the blank part all round and peel off the PET film on the back.

5

5. Prepare the wooden panel

Firstly, tack the white cloth to the wooden panel so that the wooden frame base is not visible through the printed canvas: prepare a sheet of white cloth of the same size as the printed canvas, and tack it to the panel with a tucker gun (or fix it with drawing pins).

Fix the one side at first, then fix the opposite side pulling the cloth. Fold the cloth left and tack it at each corner so that the corners look neat.

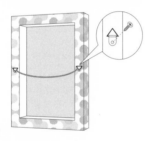

6

6. Fix the printed canvas to the frame

As you did with the white cloth, now fix the printed canvas to the panel over the white cloth.

Attach the D-hooks to the back of the panel: Select the position of the hooks and attach them with a screwdriver. Pass the string through the hooks and tie.

Now your fabric wall plaque is ready to hang!

Try hanging a few plaques in a line on a wall to create a stylish atmosphere. You could hang it near your working desk, to feel relaxed and comfortable whenever you look at it.

How to make an "original reusable bag"

By using the patterns, create a reusable bag to your own original design. This is a multi-purpose bag which you can use not only for shopping but also for holding your lunch box. If you use this bag, the number of plastic bags that end up littering the environment will be reduced.

※You can use iron-on transfer paper made by the manufacturer of your printer, or the same kind of paper sold by different manufacturers. (Choose the one suitable for your printer, such as "for Inkjet printers only"). Choose the right size of paper for your design. You can use any standard domestic iron as long as it can reach 180 – 200℃.

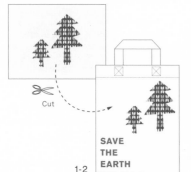

Cut

SAVE
THE
1-2   EARTH

3

○You will need:

A reusable bag, iron-on transfer paper, an iron, an ironing board and a pair of scissors

1. Create a design with the patterns

Register the pattern you would like to use in "Swatch" (see p181). Select the pattern registered in "Swatch" to paint the object you have created. You are free to design what you want-you can include letters, for example.

2. Test print on ordinary paper

Before printing on the iron-on transfer paper, print the design out on ordinary paper. Cut the design out and put on the bag to check the size and position. Modify if necessary, and repeat this process until you have the definitive design.

3. Print on the iron-on transfer paper

Print the design out on the iron-on transfer paper. Check which is the printing side of the paper, and set it on the printer. Select "File" → "Print" to show the print window, and select "Iron-on transfer paper" for the type of paper. Click "OK" and start printing (※The design will be printed in mirror image. If there is no "Iron-on transfer paper" option on your printer, you should make a mirror image of the original design beforehand).

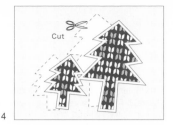

4

4. Cut it out

Once you have printed your design, cut off the blank part of the paper with scissors. Leave about 5mm of the blank part around the design for perfect results.

5. Prepare the ironing board

You should use a firm ironing board. If you don't have one, lay 15-20 sheets of newspaper on a flat, heat-resistant surface, and cover with a piece of ordinary paper or cloth bigger than the design to be printed.

5-7

6. Heat the iron

Heat the iron. Set the temperature at 180-200 ℃ with no steam. Heat the iron fully (If the iron is not hot enough, the results may be disappointing).

7. Transfer the design

Lay the bag on the ironing board with the surface to be printed on top. Place the iron-on transfer paper on top. First of all, iron lightly over the whole paper so that it sticks to the bag. Secondly, iron firmly and thoroughly. If you do not use enough pressure, the design will not transfer well and it will peel off easily later on. So put your weight behind the iron!

8

8. Peel off the iron-on transfer paper

The bag will be very hot immediately after ironing, so you wait for a couple of minutes until it cools. Peel off the iron-on transfer paper slowly starting from the edge.

Now you have your own original reusable bag!

Petit Pattern Book: Scandinavian Style
License Agreement of the Software

1. License

1) This License Agreement is a legal agreement between you (the "User"), who purchased the product Petit Pattern Book: Scandinavian Style, and BNN, Inc. ("BNN"), in respect of the attached CD-ROM entitled Petit Pattern Book: Scandinavian Style ("Software"). The User agrees to be bound by the terms of this License Agreement by installing, copying, or using the Software. BNN grants the User the right to use a copy of the Software on one personal computer for the exclusive use of the User.

2) The User may modify, edit, or combine the materials included in the Software except the cases specified in "2. Limitations"; the User has the right to use the Software principally for design of the following objects.
   ○ Digital media including websites.
   ○ Graphics for shop interiors, signs, etc.
   ○ Leaflets, flyers, posters, direct mail, catalogues, pamphlets, and other tools for advertisement or sales promotion.
   ○ Goods, clothes, greeting cards, name cards and other articles for personal production and use. (The Software may be used for personal, professional, and commercial purposes, provided that the articles produced are not offered for sale. The User may not sell articles made with the Software, even when of a personal nature. Please read the following Limitations carefully.)

2. Limitations

The User is not licensed to do any of the following:

1) Copy the Software, unless copying it is unavoidable to enable it to be used on one personal computer.
2) License, or otherwise by any means permit, any other person to use the Software.
3) Use the Software to design of products for distribution.
4) Use the Software for the commercial production of postcards, name cards, or any other articles, or sell any such articles made using the Software.
5) Provide downloading services using the Software (including greeting card services).
6) Create an environment which allows the original data to be downloaded when you show one of the Software patterns on a home page.
7) Use the Software in order to produce any software or other products for sale.
8) Acquire the copyright in any material in the Software or any object you have created using the Software.
9) Use the Software to create obscene, scandalous, abusive or slanderous works.

3. Copyright and other intellectual property

BNN or its suppliers reserves the copyright and other intellectual property rights in the Software. When specifying the User's copyright of a product made using the Software, please also write "©2006 2m09cmGRAPHICS, Inc.".

4. Exclusion of damages

In no event shall BNN be liable for any damages whatsoever (including but not limited to, damages for loss of profit or loss of data) related to the use or inability to use of the Software or use of materials in the Software.

5. Termination of this License Agreement

If the User breaches this License Agreement, BNN has the right to withdraw the User's License granted on the basis hereof.

おしゃれなパターン素材集
Petit Pattern Book

水玉・ストライプ
Dots & Stripes
ISBN：4-86100-384-9

花柄・リーフ
Flowers & Leaves
ISBN：4-86100-385-7

和・きもの柄
Japanese Style
ISBN：4-86100-390-3

おしゃれなパターン素材集
北欧・ファブリック

2006年9月25日　初版第1刷発行

アートディレクション	中山正成 (2m09cmGRAPHICS)
ブックデザイン	山際昇太 (2m09cmGRAPHICS)
パターンデザイン	2m09cmGRAPHICS
撮影アシスタント	金子りえ
翻訳	R.I.C.出版株式会社
発行人	長谷川新多郎
発行所	株式会社ビー・エヌ・エヌ新社
	〒163-1111
	東京都新宿区西新宿6-22-1　新宿スクエアタワー11F
	fax 03-3345-1127　e-mail info@bnn.co.jp
印刷・製本	株式会社 シナノ